Christmas Handcrafts
Book Four

Oxmoor
House®

Christmas Handcrafts, Book Four

©1995 by Oxmoor House, Inc.
Book Division of Southern Progress Corporation
P.O. Box 2463
Birmingham, Alabama 35201

Published by Oxmoor House, Inc., Leisure Arts, Inc., and
Symbol of Excellence Publishers, Inc.

Library of Congress Catalog Card Number: 92-60993
Hardcover ISBN: 0-8487-1469-5
Softcover ISBN: 0-8487-1470-9
ISSN: 1074-8962
Manufactured in the United States of America
First Printing 1995

Oxmoor House, Inc.

Editor-in-Chief: Nancy J. Fitzpatrick
Senior Crafts Editor: Susan Ramey Cleveland
Senior Editor, Editorial Services: Olivia Kindig Wells
Associate Production Manager: Theresa L. Beste
Production Assistant: Marianne Jordan

Symbol of Excellence Publishers, Inc.

Editor-in-Chief: Phyllis Hoffman
Executive Editor: Barbara Cockerham
Editor: Diane Kennedy-Jackson
Editorial Assistants: Susan Branch, Cindy Housel, Carol Odom
Contributing Writer: Amy Hatcher Ryan
Production Director: Perry James
Creative Director: Mac Jamieson
Executive Art Director: Yukie McLean
Art Director: Michael Whisenant
Graphic Designers: Dottie Barton, Scott Begley,
    Charles Long, Rick Nance
Photographer: David L. Maxwell
Photography Stylists: Flo Dupuy, Cathy Muir, Ada Parker,
    Glenda Parker, Tracey M. Runnion, Angie N. Sinclair,
    Jarinda Wiechman

Dear Handcrafter,

Do you love Christmas more than any other time of the year? Do you begin in January to work on the projects you want to complete in time for decorating and giving during the holiday season ahead? Well, whether you are able to plan that far ahead or you just wish that you could, we think the projects we've gathered together on the following pages are certain to inspire you to get started!

Whether your idea of the perfect day includes an unlimited amount of time for crafting, endless hours for knitting or crocheting, quiet time for cross stitching, or neighborhood gatherings for quilting, you're going to find a multitude of projects on the pages that follow that you'll want to be sure to add to your "to-make" list. From eye-catching quilting to classic crochet and cross stitch to charming craft projects—the possibilities are endless. So take a look at this glorious collection of Christmas-inspired designs, and get set for an unforgettable year of handicrafting pleasures!

Happy Holidays!

Diane Kennedy-Jackson

Contents

TREES TO REMEMBER

Each holiday season brings with it the desire to find just the right ornaments to add to our collections. On the following pages, we have assembled an array of branch trimmers—from elegant to whimsical, from cross stitch to knitting to crafting—that will add just what is needed to make your Christmas decorating complete. And you're guaranteed to have lots of fun while you're busy creating your favorites. If your penchant is for the traditional, the charming Cookie-Cutter Ornaments will be ideal! For decorating delights with a touch of the unexpected, the Ornaments from Nature collection, the one-of-a-kind Memory Ornaments, the patriotic Americana Christmas collection, or the boldly colored Victorian-Look Ornaments will be the perfect pieces for trimming your tree.

Treasures for the Tree

Among the special memories we hold of preparing for the holidays, the age-old tradition of trimming the tree is perhaps the most treasured. As we unpack boxes filled with decorations and place each tiny ornament carefully and lovingly upon a branch of the evergreen, we begin again to feel a sense of awe and wonder for this most joyous of all seasons.

Right—When it's time to deck the halls with boughs of holly, these holly-sprigged **Winter Ornaments** *will fit right in with your evergreen decor. Each ornament includes several green holly leaves and crimson berries. You can stitch the year on all of these ornaments and a name on three of them for special personalization. Charts begin on page 24.*

Opposite—Your tree will take on new style when you add these fantastic **Heartwarming Ornaments** *to your collection. Beads and ribbon combine to make the* **Paper Heart Ornaments** *Christmas decorations. Holiday-colored hearts of red, green, and gold stitched on perforated paper will glitter in the lights on your evergreen's branches. The small and large ornaments will be a joy to stitch and a pleasure to view on your Christmas tree. Also, our* **Winter Weather Ornaments** *are simple to knit from cozy-looking red and green yarn. The miniature knitted mittens, scarf, hat, and stocking have all the details of their full-size counterparts—fringes at the ends of the scarf, a pom-pom atop the hat, and tiny thumbs on the mittens. Instructions begin on page 26.*

Above—The rich look of stained glass makes these **Jewel-Tone Ornaments** a shining success. Simple crafting skills and a few materials are all you'll need to create these shimmering beauties. Won't they look spectacular on gift bottles of flavored oil and herb-infused vinegar? The quilt-square patterns and vibrant colors combine "country" and Victorian styles. Instructions begin on page 29.

***Above—**'Tis the season for homemade cookies . . . but cookies aren't the only things you can make with cookie cutters. In almost no time at all, you can turn those traditional Christmas shapes into fun, colorful,* **Cookie-Cutter Ornaments.** *What a delightful project for a few spare hours! Try a variety of ribbon colors and enjoy the results of your handiwork. Instructions are on page 30.*

Above and opposite—Decorating the tree, opposite, can be such fun! As you place each little drum, heart, apple, and clothespin soldier among the branches, the tree takes on an antique look. We decided to take our seasonal decorating a step further, above, by using our patriotic branch trimmers to add unexpected flair to the containers for homemade preserves and herbal oils. What lovely gifts—and the ornaments will be lasting treasures that will remind each recipient of the gift giver each time she hangs her little apple or heart from the branch of the Christmas tree. The designer of these patriotic pieces has put together a collection of ornaments that is easy to make—many of the pieces can be constructed from items you probably already have in your home. The drums are made from small aluminum cans, and the soldiers from clothespins that have been put on the shelf in favor of the modern electric dryer. This fun-to-make grouping will be a family favorite as kids of all ages participate in our holiday salute to America. Instructions begin on page 30.

12

Above—To make these **Memory Ornaments,** *you simply line transparent acrylic globes with pieces of paper bearing pictures that would have special meaning for the recipient, and then add trimmings to the outside of the globe. For example, for a music-loving friend, we constructed an ornament from used sheet music, adding black and gold trim to the outside. For a stamp collector, we placed a collage of cancelled stamps and envelope pieces with postmarks inside the clear globe. Use your personal creativity to design decorations that will delight those who receive them. Instructions are on page 32.*

Above—*Inspired by the yarn dolls made by our mothers and grandmothers during their childhood, these charming* **Victorian Yarn Angels** *will lend a touch of the Victorian era to your holiday tree when used as ornaments. If you prefer, finish them as party favors, place-card holders, or package toppers. They can be crafted to complement most any decorating theme by changing the ribbon and package colors! Instructions begin on page 32.*

Left—*These tiny* **Tatted Angels** *will be quick to create for those who are well-versed in the old-fashioned art of tatting. Vary the look of your angels with different threads—try metallic gold or aqua or sprinkle white angels with glitter for a truly heavenly gleam. Instructions begin on page 33.*

Right—The posh, ornate look so well-loved by the Victorians has been captured in this set of **Victorian-Look Ornaments** for the Christmas trees of today. The **Crazy-Quilt Fans** offer a use for your scraps of satin, velvet, lamé, lace, and ribbon. Place as many embellishments as you please, use different colors, and make these ornaments your unique creations. The **Crazy-Quilt Diamonds** use elaborate trims and glittery beads to achieve the Victorian look. Unique and lovely, the **Hot Air Balloon Ornaments** are sure to become your favorites. Tiny baskets filled with tinier gifts are suspended by lengths of ribbon from fabric-covered Styrofoam® balls. Choose your favorite colors and trim the "balloons" with lace, beads, ribbon bows, metallic rickrack, or whatever suits your fancy. Instructions begin on page 34.

Above, left, and opposite—
Give customary decorating an interesting twist when you make this appealing collection of heart-shaped marbled ornaments to display on your holiday tree. The designer created this collection of pastel tree trimmers and an assortment of other projects, using starch, thin paints, and a simple, yet fascinating, crafting technique. For a great gift idea, use the same method to craft bookmarks for a special friend who always has her nose buried in a book. If you've ever had trouble finding boxed cards that appeal to you, these projects will provide the ideal solution to your dilemma; and your holiday greetings to all the family members and friends on your Christmas-card list will be unforgettable! Instructions begin on page 36.

Left—It seems so appropriate to decorate an evergreen tree with ornaments made from natural ingredients. These **Ornaments from Nature** *include* **Peach Seed Flowers, Seed Stars, Watermelon Seed Wreaths, Twig Baskets, Pinecone Flowers, Flower Wreaths, Popcorn Balls, Gilded Walnuts, Floral Bouquets,** *and* **Indian Corn Balls.** *What a splendid way to continue one season into the next! By saving and drying flowers and the seeds from summer and autumn fruits and vegetables, you can enjoy a part of these seasons even after snow has added winter's blanket to the ground. If you'd like to take the natural look even further, we suggest wrapping gifts in brown paper and tying them with different-colored raffia bows. Instructions begin on page 38.*

Left—We think these **Poinsettia Ornaments** are an extremely clever way to use fabric scraps. Use bits of white fabric to cover the Styrofoam® ball, and then cut petals from red and green scraps to create the vivid poinsettias on the face of each ornament. Gold beads add sparkle to the flower centers, and red ribbon bows and hanging loops top each ornament. These simple, pretty decorations are fun to craft with children who "don't have anything to do" during the days before Christmas. Instructions are on page 28.

Opposite—Remember those snippets of yarn that you didn't want to throw away, because you were sure you'd find a use for them? Well, here's the perfect opportunity—the **Tiny Treasures Stockings** give you the chance to put your scraps of yarn to good use. You may see the bottom of your work-basket for the first time in years! Only the smallest presents will fit inside these darling stockings, but they make adorable ornaments and are sure to spark comments from all who see them. Instructions begin on page 27.

Winter Ornaments

DMC	Marlitt	Color
8 817		coral red, vy. dk.
9 349		coral, dk.
○ white		white
╱ 311		navy, med.
X 986		forest, vy. dk.
⌢ 989		forest
• 310		black
■ 347		salmon, dk.
‐ 350		coral, med.
bs	white	white

Fabrics: *Cap* and *Mitten*–18-count white Aida from Charles Craft, Inc.; *Stocking* and *Snowman*–22-count white Hardanger from Charles Craft, Inc.

Stitch count:

Cap	47H x 54W
Mitten	54H x 42W
Stocking	53H x 41W
Snowman	49H x 29W

Design size:

Cap
14-count	3⅜" x 3⅞"
16-count	3" x 3⅜"
18-count	2⅝" x 3"
22-count	4¼" x 5"

Mitten
14-count	3⅞" x 3"
16-count	3⅜" x 2⅝"
18-count	3" x 2⅓"
22-count	5" x 3⅞"

Stocking
14-count	3¾" x 3"
16-count	3⅓" x 2½"
18-count	3" x 2¼"
22-count	4⅞" x 3¾"

Snowman
14-count	3½" x 2"
16-count	3" x 1⅞"
18-count	2¾" x 1⅝"
22-count	4½" x 2⅝"

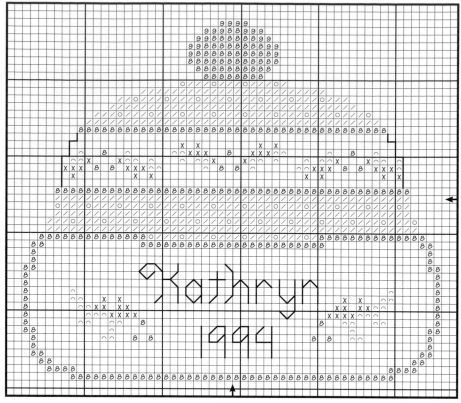

CAP

Instructions:

Cap and *Mitten:* Cross stitch using two strands of floss. Backstitch (bs) using one strand of floss.

Stocking and *Snowman:* Cross stitch over two threads, using three strands of floss. Backstitch (bs) using two strands of floss unless otherwise indicated.

Note: To personalize ornaments, use alphabet provided.

Backstitch (bs) instructions:

Cap
310	name and year
311	holly border edges

Mitten
310	name and year
311	mitten edges

Stocking
310	name and year
311	stocking edges
Marlitt	snowflakes (one strand)

Snowman
817	mouth
986	year
310	remainder of backstitching

Materials:
⅛ yd. 44/45"-wide white fabric (for backing)

BLANKET STITCH

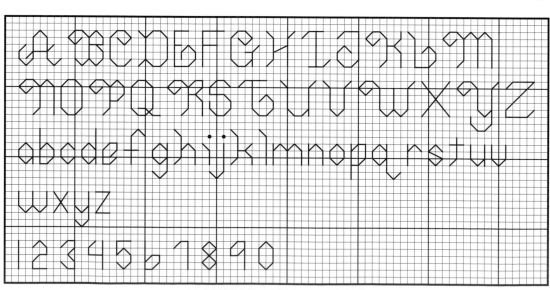

ALPHABET AND NUMERALS

24

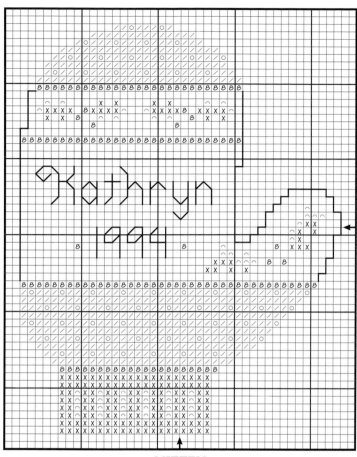

MITTEN

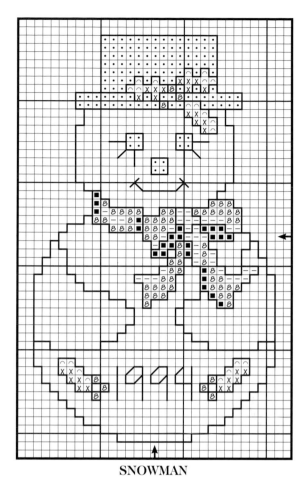

SNOWMAN

⅛ yd. 44/45"-wide white flannel
Dritz® Fray Check™
8" length ⅛"-wide white satin ribbon
 (for hanger)
Scissors

Note: Materials listed will make one *Winter Ornament.*

1. Complete stitching following instructions given.
2. Cut around outside edge of stitched design, leaving ⅜" cross-stitch fabric beyond edge of stitching.
3. Cut a backing piece the same size as stitched piece from white fabric. Repeat with white flannel.
4. Apply Fray Check™ around outside edges of stitched piece and backing piece. Let dry.
5. Layer backing, flannel, and stitched piece together.
6. Work blanket stitch around perimeter, using two strands white embroidery floss. Weave ends of floss into center of ornament and clip floss tails.
7. Fold 8" length of ribbon in half and tack fold at top center of ornament. Tie ribbon ends in a knot to form hanger or use ribbon to tie ornaments to tree or wreath, tying ribbon in a bow.

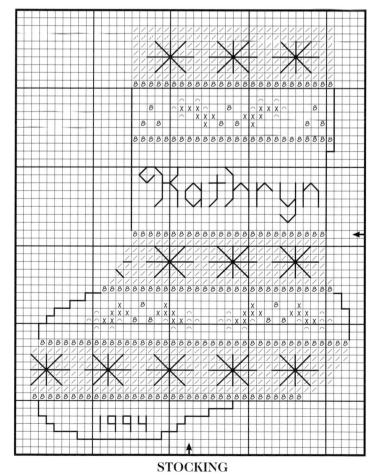

STOCKING

Heartwarming Ornaments

Large Paper Heart Ornaments

Kreinik
1/16"
Ribbon   Color
Red Ornament
- ■ 009HL   Emerald
- • 032   Pearl

White Ornament
- ■ 009HL   Emerald
- • 031   Crimson

Mill Hill Seed Beads
Red Ornament
- ♡ 332   Emerald
- X 557   Gold
- ○ 557   Gold

White Ornament
- ♡ 332   Emerald
- X 557   Gold
- ○ 367   Garnet

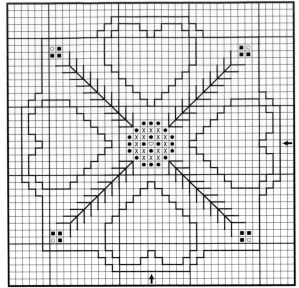

LARGE PAPER HEART ORNAMENT

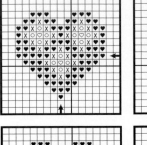
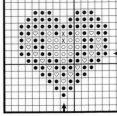
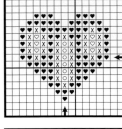
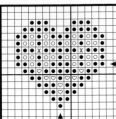
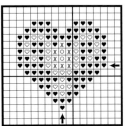
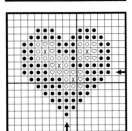

SMALL PAPER HEART ORNAMENTS

Materials: 14-count red or white perforated paper, sewing thread to match beads
Stitch count: 35H x 35W
Design size:
14-count   2¾" x 2¾"

Instructions: Work designs in half-cross stitch. Attach beads with half-cross stitches, using sewing thread. Backstitch pine boughs, using one strand 009HL.

Small Paper Heart Ornaments

Kreinik
1/16"
Ribbon   Color
- ♥ 031   Crimson
- • 032   Pearl

Mill Hill Seed Beads
- ♡ 332   Emerald
- ○ 367   Garnet
- X 557   Gold

Materials: 14-count red or white perforated paper, sewing thread to match beads
Stitch count: 13H x 13W
Design size:
14-count   1" x 1"

Instructions: Work designs in half-cross stitch, stitching hearts with crimson ribbon background on white perforated paper and hearts with pearl ribbon background on red perforated paper. Attach beads with half-cross stitches, using sewing thread.

Finishing instructions
Materials:
9" x 12" sheet 14-count red perforated paper
9" x 12" sheet 14-count white perforated paper
Hand-sewing needle
Sharp scissors **or** craft knife

Note: Materials listed will make one *Large Paper Heart Ornament* and three *Small Paper Heart Ornaments* on red perforated paper and one *Large Paper Heart Ornament* and three *Small Paper Heart Ornaments* on white perforated paper.

1. Complete stitching following instructions given.
2. Cut out around perimeter of each design, using sharp scissors **or** craft knife, cutting one square beyond stitching, and leaving additional squares in tight corners. Refer to photo on page **9**. Set aside.
3. Cut three 1½" squares from red perforated paper and three 1½" squares from white perforated paper for backings for *Small Paper Heart Ornaments*. Cut one 3¼" square from red perforated paper and one 3¼" square from white perforated paper for backings for *Large Paper Heart Ornaments*.
4. To make hanger for each ornament, thread needle with 1/16" ribbon in color to match paper. Begin on back side of ornament and bring needle through to front side through hole just left of the center, leaving a tail on back side of ornament. Return to back side through next

hole to the right, leaving a loop on front of ornament, and tie braid ends in a knot on back side of ornament to secure.
5. Center each motif on a perforated paper backing piece, aligning holes. Work running stitch near edge of design through both layers of paper, using ribbon color to match paper. Trim edges of perforated paper backing even with ornament front.

Winter Weather Ornaments

Materials:
Coats & Clark Red Heart® Super Sport Yarn Art. E271 3-oz. skeins: 1 skein **each** #918 vermillion (A) and #687 paddy green (B)
Four size 1 (2.25mm) double-pointed knitting needles (dpn)
Size 1 (2.25mm) knitting needles
Size 2/C (2.75mm) aluminum crochet hook
Tapestry needle

Gauge: In St st and color pat, 8 sts = 1"; 10 rows = 1"

Notes: *Mittens* are worked with dpn, knitting every rnd for St st. *Stocking, Hat,* and *Scarf* are worked back and forth in St st with straight needles. When working with two colors, bring new color from under previous color for a twist to prevent holes. Carry unused strand loosely across WS of work.

26

Cut and join as necessary. When working from chart, read chart from bottom to top and from left to right for wrong-side or p rows, and from right to left for right-side or k rows.

Hat

Note: When working hat from chart, work from C to G for RS rows and from G to C for WS rows.
Beg at lower edge, CO 31 sts with A.
Rows 1 & 2: K for Garter st border.
Row 3 (WS): P.
Rows 4–8: In St st, follow chart rows 1–5.
Rows 9–11: Work with A in St st.
Row 12: K 1; * k 2 tog across—16 sts.
Rows 13, 15, & 17: P.
Row 14: K 2 tog across—8 sts.
Row 16: K 2 tog across—4 sts.
Cut yarn, leaving a 10" tail. Thread tail into tapestry needle and back through rem 4 sts; pull up tightly to gather. With same tail, sew back seam.
Pom-pom: Wrap B 25 times around two fingers. With a separate strand, tie through lps on one end. Clip lps on other end and trim to shape. Tie at top of hat.
Hanging loop: With crochet hook and RS facing, attach A ½" from top of hat at seam with sl st, ch 12, and sl st in joining.

Scarf

Note: When working scarf from chart, work from C to D for RS rows and D to C for WS rows.
With A, CO 11 sts.
Rows 1 & 2: K.
Row 3 (WS): Keeping 2 sts each edge in Garter st throughout project, p across.
Rows 4–8: Beg with a k row, follow chart on center 7 sts.

Rows 9–13: Work with A in St st for 5 rows.
Rep rows 4–13 for color pat 6 times more. Work rows 1–5 of chart once more, then with A, p 2 rows, k 1 row. BO all sts.
Fringe: Cut 24 strands B, **each** 3" long. Holding 2 strands tog, fold in half to form a lp. With crochet hook, attach at each end of scarf by drawing lp through one st and pulling ends through lp. Tighten to form a knot. Attach 6 double strands at each end. Trim to 1".
Finishing: Make a lp with scarf, having ends extend 2" beyond base of lp. Sl st on back side to secure. At top of loop, make hanging loop as for *Hat*.

Stocking

Note: When working stocking from chart, work from D to G for RS rows and from G to D for WS rows.
Beg at top edge, CO 25 sts with A.
Rows 1 & 2: K.
Row 3 (WS): P.
Rows 4–19: Work in St st following chart, beginning with row 1.
Heel shaping: K 8, turn, sl 1, p 7, turn; k 7, turn, sl 1, p 6, turn; k 6, turn, sl 1, p 5, turn; k 5, turn, sl 1, p 4, turn; k 4, turn, sl 1, p 3, turn; k 3, turn, sl 1, p 2, turn; k across all 25 sts. P 8, turn, sl 1, k 7, turn; p 7, turn, sl 1, k 6, turn; p 6, turn, sl 1, k 5, turn; p 5, turn, sl 1, k 5, turn; p 4, turn, sl 1, k 3, turn; p 3, turn, sl 1, k 2, turn; p across all 25 sts.
Following chart from row 17, work 3 rows even.
Continue working from chart while shaping as follows: (RS) K 1, sl 1, k 1, psso, k to end. (WS) P 1, p 2 tog, p to end. Rep these 2 shaping rows 5 more times—13 sts.
Cut yarn, leaving a 10" tail. Thread tail into tapestry needle and gather toe and sew back seam. Make a hanging lp as for *Hat*.

Mittens (Make two.)

Note: When working mittens from chart, work around every rnd from C to E.
With A, CO 18 sts. Divide sts with 6 sts on each of 3 dpn. Join and with 4th dpn, p 2 rnds. K 1 rnd.
Follow chart and rep across, k 5 rnds.
Thumb: K 2 sts; with small amount of contrasting yarn, k the nxt 3 sts. Transfer these sts back to the left-hand needle and k with A. Continue working from rnd 6 of chart through rnd 13.
Rnd 14: With A, k 2 tog around—9 sts.
Rnd 15: (K 1, k 2 tog) around—6 sts.
Cut yarn, leaving a 10" tail. Thread tail into tapestry needle; gather and fasten.
Finishing: Remove contrasting yarn from thumb sts and place on needle.

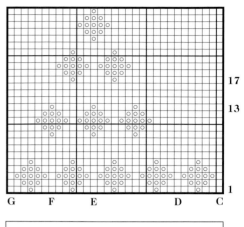

			17
			13
			1
G	F	E	D C

□ = A	○ = B

With A, pick up and k 3 sts on row above opening—6 sts. K 6 rnds. K 2 tog around—3 sts.
Cut yarn, leaving a 10" tail. With tapestry needle, thread end through rem sts, gather, and fasten.
After completing second mitten, with the RS facing, attach A at thumb edge, and with crochet hook, make a 4" chain. Sl st to first mitten at thumb edge and fasten off. Weave in loose ends.

Tiny Treasures Stockings

Materials:
1 skein **each** color fingering-weight yarn, colors: red, burgundy, dark green, white
1 skein white angora
12" length ⅜"-wide complementary satin ribbon for **each** ornament (for hanger)
½–1 oz. fingering-weight cotton **or** rayon (for waste yarn)
Set of 5 double-pointed knitting needles, size 1
Tapestry needle in size needed to accommodate yarn

Two ½" red pom-poms
Stitch markers
Scissors

Note: Materials listed will make one pair of **each** different type of *Tiny Treasures Stockings.*

Long, Striped Sock

Stripe pattern: 3 rnds dark green, 2 rnds burgundy, 1 rnd white, 2 rnds burgundy. Repeat last 8 rnds for pattern.

With dark green, CO 32 stitches. Divide stitches onto four needles, having 8 sts on each needle. Join and place a marker. Work 4 rnds in k1, p1, ribbing. Work 26 rnds in stripe pattern.

Heel placement round: Drop main-color yarn and knit across the first two needles, using an 18" length of waste yarn. End off waste yarn, leaving a 3" tail. Return to first needle, pick up main-color yarn and knit across the two needles just worked with waste yarn. Finish rnd. K 13 more rnds, keeping in stripe pattern. Fasten off burgundy and white yarn. Continue with dark green.

Toe:

Rnd 1: k.

Rnd 2: * k1, sl st 1, k1, psso, k to end of needle, k to last 3 sts on nxt needle, k2 tog, k1, * rep once.

Rep rnds 1 and 2 until 2 sts rem on each needle, ending at marker. Weave sts of toe together with Kitchener stitch.

Note: The Kitchener stitch is sometimes called "weaving the toe." To work, slip toe sts to one double-pointed needle and foot sts to another double-pointed needle. Thread approximately 1 yd. of yarn into tapestry needle. Holding needles parallel, with wrong sides of stocking together, with sts at right edge of needles, and leaving short tail to be woven in later, * insert tapestry needle into first st of front needle as if to k, and sl st off needle. Insert tapestry needle into second st of front needle as if to p, and draw yarn through, leaving st on needle. Insert tapestry needle into first st on back needle as if to p, and remove st from needle. Insert tapestry needle into second st on back as if to k, and draw yarn through. Rep from * until one st remains on each needle. Draw yarn through st on front needle as if to k and through st on back needle as if to p. Remove double-pointed needles. Weave in ends. Turn sock inside-out and weave in all ends.

Heel: Remove waste yarn, picking up upper open loops on one needle and lower open loops on another needle as waste yarn is removed.

Rnd 1: With dark green yarn, leave a 3" tail. *Pick up 1 st in sp between needles. K across 8 sts. With second needle k across rem 8 sts on needle and pick up 1 st in sp, * rep once, using third and fourth needles.

Note: There are now 36 sts divided equally on four needles. Beg with rnd 2, work heel as for toe until four sts rem on each needle. Divide rem 16 sts onto two needles and weave together as for toe.

Angora-Trimmed Sock

CO 32 sts with dark green. Join and place a marker. Drop dark green. P 3 rnds with angora. Work rem of sock as for *Long, Striped Sock,* using red yarn for heel and toe.

Crew Sock

Work as for *Long, Striped Sock* with the following changes:

1. CO in white. Work in a k2, p2 pattern for 3 rnds.
2. With burgundy, rib 2 rnds. Fasten off burgundy.
3. With white, rib 3 rnds.
4. With dark green, rib 2 rnds. Fasten off dark green.
5. With white, rib 19 rnds.
6. With white, k 3 rnds.
7. Following directions from heel placement round, finish sock in white, as for *Long, Striped Sock.*

Short, Striped Anklet

Stripe pattern: * k1 rnd burgundy, 1 rnd dark green, 1 rnd red, rep from * for stripe pattern.

Using red yarn, CO 32 sts and work as for *Long, Striped Sock.* When ribbing is completed k 2 rnds. Work 19 rnds in stripe pattern, then work heel placement round. Continue as for *Long, Striped Sock,* using plain red yarn for heel and toe.

Ladies' Sport Sock

With white, CO 28 sts. Work 3 rnds of k1, p1 ribbing. On nxt rnd, increase 1 st on each needle (32 sts). K 2 rnds. Work heel placement round and rem of sock as for *Long, Striped Sock.*

To finish: With red yarn and tapestry needle, work 1 rnd of blanket stitch around top of sock. Tack red pom-pom to back of sock.

To finish as ornaments: Cut 12" length of ribbon in half and tack one end of each ribbon length at top center on either side of ornament. Tie ribbon in a bow 1"–2" above top of ornament, forming a hanging loop with a bow at the top.

Poinsettia Ornaments

Materials:
2½" STYROFOAM brand plastic foam ball
Small scraps cotton fabric, colors: red, white, green
Mod Podge® matte-mat
16" length ⅛"-wide red satin ribbon
3" length white fabric-covered wire (for hanger)
12–14 small gold beads
½" paintbrush
Tacky glue
Scissors
Ice pick **or** small nail

Note: Materials listed will make one *Poinsettia Ornament.*

1. Cut white fabric into ¾"- to 1"-square pieces. Apply Mod Podge® to small area of ball, place a piece of fabric over area, and brush more Mod Podge® over fabric. Add second piece fabric in same manner, overlapping first piece slightly. Continue until ball is completely covered. Let dry.
2. Cut six pieces from green fabric and six pieces from red fabric, using large pattern. Cut six pieces from red fabric, using small pattern. Apply Mod Podge® to back side of green pieces and place evenly on ball, forming a circle, with pointed ends meeting in center. Place large red pieces between green pieces in same manner. Use small red pieces to overlap green piece and large red pieces. Apply one to two coats Mod Podge® over entire design to be sure all edges are glued down. Let dry.
3. Apply small dots of glue in center of design and add beads. Let dry.
4. To prepare ball for hanger, stick small holes approximately ¼" apart in top of ball, using ice pick or small nail. Bend wire into a "U" shape, apply glue to wire ends, and insert ends into ball.
5. Cut 8" length from ribbon and thread through wire. Tie ribbon ends together to form hanger. Tie remainder of ribbon into a bow and glue to top of ornament near wire.

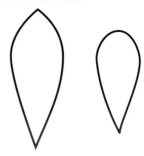

ORNAMENT PATTERNS

Jewel-Tone Ornaments

Note: For these projects, a general materials list has been given. Specific materials for each project have been listed separately.

General materials:
3" square 3/16"-thick white foamcore board
14" length ¼"-wide green satin ribbon
26" length ¼"-wide red- and metallic-gold trim **or** 13" length ½"-wide metallic-gold trim
1 yd. 1/16"-wide metallic-gold cord
Two 3" squares medium-weight acrylic plastic (**Note:** Acrylic-plastic sheets are available in some stationery stores.)
4" square green felt
8½" x 11" sheet white paper
8½" x 11" piece corrugated cardboard
Small scrap cardboard at least 4" square (for pattern)
½ skein DMC six-strand cotton embroidery floss, color: 321 red
Silver glitter
Tacky glue
Liner paintbrush
3" or larger plastic triangle
Metal ruler
Craft stick
Scissors
Heavy-duty craft knife
Fine sandpaper
Toothpicks
Waxed paper
Paper towels
Pencil
Cutting board

Note: General materials listed will make one *Jewel-Tone Ornament.*

Patch Star Ornament
Materials:
3" Iron-On Fabric Silhouette Quilt Square (**Note:** Designer used *Patch Star,* No. F603 from Tree Toys.)
Gallery Glass™ waterbase transparent glass paints, colors: Kelly Green, Harvest Red, Sunny Yellow

Grandma's Fan Ornament
Materials:
3" Iron-On Fabric Silhouette Quilt Square (**Note:** Designer used *Grandma's Fan,* No. F602 from Tree Toys.)
Gallery Glass™ waterbase transparent glass paints, colors: Kelly Green, Harvest Red, Sunny Yellow, Amethyst

Note: Both quilt-square ornaments are made following the same procedure. The instructions given are for one ornament. Use photo as a guide for applying transparent paints, or substitute colors of your choice.

1. Draw 3" square atop cardboard to make pattern, using sharp pencil and plastic triangle to ensure accuracy and square corners. Before cutting, check accuracy of pattern against fabric silhouette quilt square and adjust pattern as needed. Place cardboard atop cutting board and cut out pattern, using craft knife and metal ruler.
2. Outline one 3" square on foamcore board, using sharp pencil and pattern. Cut out square atop cutting board, using craft knife and metal ruler. When cutting, hold knife blade at right angle to cutting board. **Do not** slant knife blade. Lightly smooth edges with sandpaper. Lightly sand one side (front) of foamcore square and spread that side with thick layer of glue, using craft stick. Sprinkle with glitter and press lightly with finger to embed glitter into glue. Let dry atop waxed paper.
3. Cut two 3" squares from acrylic plastic by holding pattern tightly on plastic and cutting around pattern, using scissors. Clean plastic with water and paper towels to remove fingerprints.
4. Apply fine (1/32"), even bead of tacky glue to edge around perimeter of one plastic square, using toothpick. (**Note:** Hold square in center between thumb and forefinger and rotate square as you glue.) Remove paper from back of silhouette and adhere fusible side of fabric to glued side of plastic square, using toothpick to lightly tap glued edges together. (**Note:** Avoid smearing or squeezing glue beyond narrow edge.) Apply fine bead of glue to right side of fabric square in same manner and glue second plastic square atop silhouette. Again, avoid squeezing glue beyond narrow edge. Let dry atop waxed paper.
5. To assemble painting and drying tray, place sheet of white paper atop corrugated cardboard. Cover with waxed paper. When glued quilt square is dry enough to handle, place quilt square right-side down (fusible-side up) atop waxed paper. Using photo on page **10** as a guide for color placement, flow transparent paints onto plastic within areas where white shows through, using paintbrush and covering areas heavily. (**Note:** Since it will not be seen from front, extend each color slightly beyond edges to ensure coverage but

do not allow colors to run together. If large bubbles appear in paint, break with toothpick. Small bubbles will not show.) Without tilting tray, set silhouette aside to dry for four hours or more.
6. Brush away excess glitter from atop foamcore square. Apply a thin coat of glue to back of foamcore square, using craft stick, and firmly press glued side onto felt square. Trim excess felt from edges, using scissors. Let dry.
7. When paints have dried, place beading of tacky glue along edges of plastic square. (**Note:** Also place a small mound of glue at each of the four corners of star square and at diagonal, unpainted corners of fan square.) Glue painted side of plastic square to glittered side of foamcore square. Press two pieces together firmly, allowing glitter to illuminate transparent paints.
8. Attach one row of metallic-gold cord to front of ornament along edge of plastic, using fine bead of tacky glue. Glue one side at a time and cut at end before gluing next side. Embed and straighten cord in glue, using clean toothpick. Let dry.
9. To make tassel, leave entire skein of floss intact and divide strands in half, clipping strands to separate. Set aside one half-skein. Fold remaining half-skein, with which you are working, in half, forming a loop. At fold, slip 5" length of metallic-gold cord beneath loop and double knot cord tightly around floss, referring to illustration. Straighten floss strands, making sure knot is at top. Hold strands together firmly and wrap metallic cord tightly around strands three times, ½" below fold. As you wrap, end of cord will be secured. Cut away excess cord, allowing approximately ⅛" excess. Tuck excess cord under wrapped cord, using tip of scissors. Secure with dot of glue.
10. To glue tassel to ornament, open metallic cord ends at top of tassel to form a "V," and trim each end to 1¼". Place ornament right-side up, turning it to form a diamond as pictured. Glue

ILLUSTRATION

"V" ends of cord from tassel to bottom corner of ornament. Embed ends into glue several times while glue dries, using toothpick.

11. Glue green ribbon along edge of ornament, beginning and ending at tassel. As you glue, be sure you are covering raw edges on back of ornament by butting ribbon and felt together. Glue two rows ¼"-wide metallic trim (or one row ½"-wide trim) around four edges atop ribbon in same manner, making sure raw edges on front are covered. Apply extra dab of glue on trim ends to prevent raveling. Embed trim into glue several times while glue dries, using toothpick.

12. To finish, fold 10" length of metallic-gold cord in half to form hanger. Wrap cut ends together around finger and pull through to form a knot approximately 1½" from ends. Glue knot to felt, placing knot near top of ornament.

Cookie-Cutter Ornaments

Materials:
Assorted metal cookie cutters (**Note:** Designer used stars, evergreen trees, bells, candles, angels, snowmen, candy canes, and strawberries, which resemble outdoor bulbs.)
Small, dried flowers in assorted colors of your choice
Tacky glue
Toothpicks (for applying glue)
⅞"-wide red grosgrain ribbon (**Note:** To determine amount of ribbon needed, add inside and outside perimeter measurements plus 1" for **each** cookie cutter.)
9" length ¼"-wide red satin ribbon for **each** ornament
8" length metallic-gold thread for **each** ornament (for hanger)
Measuring tape
Hand-sewing needle
Scissors
Hot glue gun and glue sticks

1. Cut ⅞"-wide ribbon to fit inside perimeter of cookie cutter plus ½". Apply tacky glue to wrong side of ribbon along one end and approximately 1" down each side, using toothpick to apply glue. Press ribbon inside cookie cutter. Continue applying glue and pressing ribbon in place until inside perimeter of cookie cutter is covered. Cover outside perimeter of cookie cutter, using same method. Let dry.

2. Glue flowers inside cookie cutters as desired, referring to photo on page 11 for placement.

3. Tie ¼"-wide ribbon around top center of each cookie cutter and tie ribbon into a bow. Glue to cookie cutter to secure.

4. Thread needle with gold thread, stitch through center of bow, and tie a knot in thread ends to form hanger.

Americana Christmas

Wooden Apples
Materials:
Apple-shaped wooden cutouts with hole in stem (available at craft stores)
#4 paintbrush
#10 paintbrush
Ceramcoat® paints by Delta, colors: Tompte Red, Kelly, Brown iron oxide
7" length metallic-gold thread (for **each** hanger)
Extra-fine sandpaper
Scissors

1. Sand wooden cutouts.

2. Paint stems brown and leaves Kelly, using #4 paintbrush. Paint apples red, using #10 paintbrush. Let dry thoroughly. Sand apples lightly and down to the wood along some of the edges to give them a weathered look.

3. Insert 7" length of metallic-gold thread through hole in each apple stem and tie a knot in thread ends to form hanger.

Flag Hearts
Materials:
3" square ⅛"-thick wood (for **each** heart) **or** wooden heart cutouts (available at craft stores)
Ceramcoat® paints by Delta, colors: Tompte Red, White, Midnight, Brown iron oxide
#4 paintbrush
#10 paintbrush
7" length metallic-gold thread (for **each** hanger)
Extra-fine sandpaper
Graphite paper
Scissors
Pencil
Hammer
Small nail
Scroll saw

1. Cut out heart pattern. Trace around perimeter of pattern on wood, using graphite paper. Cut out and sand wooden heart.

2. Place pattern atop heart and trace stars-and-stripes design, using graphite paper.

3. Paint corner Midnight and stripes Tompte Red and White, using #4 paintbrush and referring to photo on page 13.

Dip end of brush handle in White and tap dots on Midnight. Paint edge and back of heart Tompte Red, using #10 paintbrush. Let dry. Sand lightly.

4. Mix a little water with Brown iron oxide, and apply a light wash over heart. Let dry.

5. Using hammer and small nail, punch a hole at top center of heart. Insert 7" length of metallic-gold thread through hole and tie a knot in thread ends to form hanger.

Drums
Materials:
8 Vienna sausage cans, empty, washed, with labels removed
3¾" yds. ¼"-thick red macramé cord
8½ yds. small gold cord
1½ yds. metallic-gold thread, cut into 7" lengths (for hangers)
Ninety-six ¼" gold beads
Ceramcoat® acrylic paint, color: Midnight
Ceramcoat® Water Base Satin Varnish
#10 paintbrush
8½" x 11" sheet cream-colored parchment paper
Sandpaper
Scissors
Thick tacky glue
Toothpicks
Pencil
Hand-sewing needle
Cooking oil

Note: Materials listed will make eight *Drums*.

1. Sand and paint can using Midnight. Let dry. Apply second coat. Let dry. Apply a coat of varnish. Let dry.

2. Apply glue along top and bottom edges of can, using toothpick. Place red cord over glue. Let dry.

3. Glue six beads along top cord, spacing evenly around can. Glue six beads along bottom cord, spacing evenly between top beads. Refer to photo on page 13 for placement.

4. Cut a 38" length of gold cord. Beginning at top and working around drum in a counterclockwise direction, wrap cord counterclockwise around top bead, then clockwise around bottom bead. Continue in this manner all the way around the drum. Tie cord ends together and trim away excess.
Note: It may be necessary to put a small amount of glue behind each bead to hold the cord as you work.

5. Cut out pattern for top of drum. Place pattern atop cream-colored parchment paper, trace around pattern, and cut out. Make eight drum tops. Apply a

small amount of glue around inside rim of can. Press paper along edge to secure. When glue is dry, paint a thin coat of cooking oil over paper. Wipe off excess.
6. Thread needle with 7" length of metallic-gold thread, sew through red cord, and tie a knot in thread ends to form hanger.

Fabric Hearts
Materials:
10" length 44/45"-wide red-white-and-blue fabric of your choice
Nine 4½" squares quilt batting
1¾" yds. metallic-gold thread, cut into 7" lengths (for hangers)
Paper and pencil
Hand-sewing needle
Scissors
Sewing machine (optional)

Note: Fabric yardage listed will make nine *Fabric Hearts*.

1. Trace heart pattern onto paper and cut out. Place paper pattern atop fabric, trace around pattern, and cut out. Make eighteen fabric hearts.
2. Layer two fabric hearts with right sides together atop batting square. Stitch through all layers, using a ¼" seam allowance and leaving an opening for turning. Trim, clip curves, turn, and slip stitch opening closed.
3. Thread needle with 7" length of metallic-gold thread, stitch through center top of heart, and tie a knot in thread ends to form hanger.

Clothespin Soldiers
Materials:
12 wooden clothespins (see note)
Twelve ¾" black acrylic pom-poms
2⅓ yds. narrow gold braid **or** cord
Ceramcoat® paints by Delta, colors: Black, Crimson, Fleshtone, Mocha, Midnight
#4 paintbrush
Liner brush (for eyes and mouth)
2⅓ yds. metallic-gold thread, cut into 7" lengths (for hangers)
Fine sandpaper
Craft glue
Hand-sewing needle
Scissors

Note: Materials listed will make twelve *Clothespin Soldiers*. To make these ornaments, you will need the old-fashioned, slide-on clothespins, as opposed to the hinged, clip-on variety commonly used today.

1. Sand clothespins. Paint top section (head) Fleshtone. Paint upper ¾" (shirt)

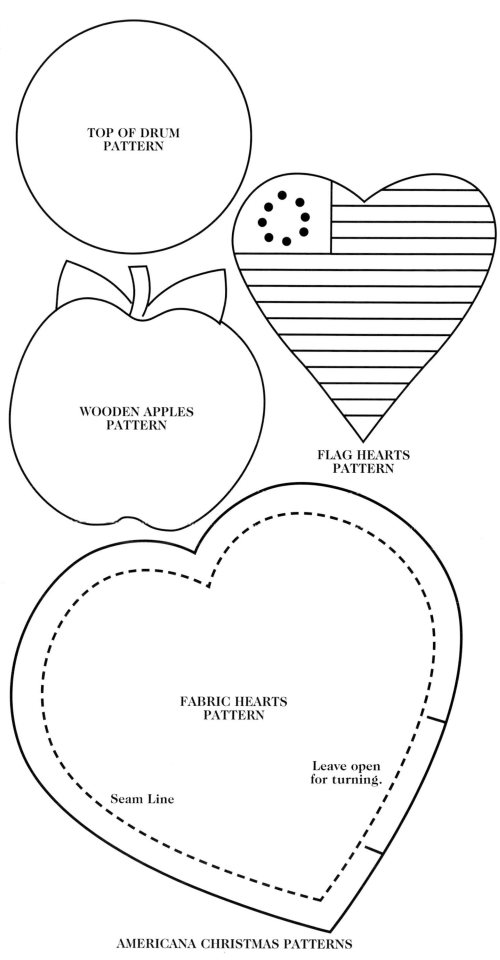

TOP OF DRUM PATTERN

WOODEN APPLES PATTERN

FLAG HEARTS PATTERN

FABRIC HEARTS PATTERN

Leave open for turning.

Seam Line

AMERICANA CHRISTMAS PATTERNS

Red. Paint bottom ¼" (shoes) Black. Paint remainder Midnight. Let paint dry between application of each color.

2. Paint hair area Mocha. Paint eyes and mouth black. Let dry.

3. Cut two pieces of gold cord each 2¼" long. Glue ends at waist front, cross in front and back, and glue remaining ends to waist back. Cut 2" piece of gold cord for belt and glue around waist, overlapping ends on back side and trimming away excess cord as needed. Refer to photo on page **13** for placement of cord.

4. Glue pom-pom to top of head and let dry.

5. Thread needle with 7" length of metallic-gold thread, sew through pom-pom, and tie a knot in thread ends to form hanger.

Memory Ornaments

Materials:

Snap-side clear acrylic globes in shapes and sizes of your choice

Fabricraft™ Multi-purpose Fabric and Craft Finish

Medium-weight decorative paper (to cover inside of **each** globe)

Decorative trim (to fit around perimeter of **each** globe)

8"–10" length matching **or** contrasting decorative trim for **each** globe (for hanger)

Scissors

Craft knife

Soft lint-free cloth

Damp sponge

Liquid seam sealant

Low-temperature glue gun and glue sticks **or** craft cement

8"–10" length decorative trim for **each** globe (optional, for bow)

Small flowers **or** fruits (optional)

Acrylic paint and medium paintbrush (optional)

Note: Suggested decorative papers include road maps, greeting cards, sheet music, playing cards, stamps on paper, color photocopies of photographs, paper bags, recipe flyers, and gift wrap. Suggested trims include ribbon, cording, braid, gathered lace, rattail cord, twine, string pearls, and yarn.

1. Open globe and separate halves. Wipe both sides of each half with a lint-free cloth to remove dust.

2. Select paper to be used. If using photocopies with black ink, take caution when applying to globe as ink may smear. (**Note:** Very fragile papers such as newsprint or magazine pages may fall apart when dampened. To add stability, adhere page to a piece of bond paper, using a thin coat of craft finish and letting dry before using.) To use greeting cards or playing cards, gently split paper plies at a corner and peel away top layer for applying to globe.

3. Choose main paper image as you would like it to appear in center front of globe. Gently tear away paper surrounding image (set torn pieces aside to use later). Carefully spread a light, even coat of craft finish over printed side of the image, using damp sponge or fingertip. Press paper, sticky-side down, to the inside center of one globe half. Rub back and forth gently, applying light pressure until paper adheres firmly and is free of deep wrinkles and bubbles.

Note: Small wrinkles may remain but are necessary for image to cling to contours of globe—these will diminish as additional layers of paper and finish are added.

4. To fill in remainder of globe front, tear pieces of paper 1" or smaller. Apply pieces to inside front of globe until covered, using craft finish and technique used for main image. Repeat for globe back.

Note: If desired, paint inside back with acrylic paint instead of covering with paper.

5. Snap globe sides together loosely to check fit. If any paper impedes closing, open globe, trim paper using craft knife, and close again to check fit. Open globe and coat all paper-covered areas with a light, even coat of fabric medium. Let dry several hours or overnight.

6. Snap globe halves together securely. Referring to photo on page **14**, glue trim over seam, beginning and ending at center top. Insert trim for hanger through loop on globe top and then knot trim ends to secure.

7. Glue on bows, flowers, or fruits to decorate globe, if desired. Apply seam sealant to cut ends of trim to prevent fraying.

Victorian Yarn Angels

Materials:

30 yds. 4-ply ecru worsted-weight yarn (for ornament) **or** 38 yds. of same (for party favor or place-card holder)

⅔ yd. 1⅜"-wide ecru/mauve lace ribbon

12" length ¼"-wide mauve satin ribbon

5" white chenille stem (pipe cleaner)

4½" metallic-gold tinsel stem

8" length metallic-gold cord (for hanger)

One 1" square purchased mauve gift package (available at craft stores)

2 ft. 30-gauge white cloth-covered wire

One 3½ oz. (2¼" high) white disposable plastic drinking cup (for **each** party favor or place-card holder)

4" x 6" piece corrugated cardboard

Low-temperature glue gun and glue sticks

Scissors

Ruler

Wire cutters

Note: *Victorian Yarn Angels* can be made as ornaments or as party favors or place-card holders. Materials listed will make one *Victorian Yarn Angel*. Steps 9–11 convert ornament to party favor/place-card holder.

1. Wind yarn smoothly 75 times around cardboard, being careful not to stretch or tangle it. Begin and end yarn at bottom edge B of cardboard, which will become angel's skirt. (See Illustration 1.)

2. To form angel's head, slip 6" length of yarn under wound yarn at top edge A of cardboard, cinching wound yarn tightly. Knot 6" length of yarn twice. Trim yarn ends close to knots. Slip yarn

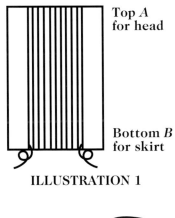

Top *A* for head

Bottom *B* for skirt

ILLUSTRATION 1

ILLUSTRATION 2

ILLUSTRATION 3

VICTORIAN YARN ANGELS ILLUSTRATIONS

off cardboard, keeping strands straight. Cut 10" length of cloth-covered wire and bend into a "U" shape. Approximately 1½" below knot, slide "U"-shaped wire around wound yarn, cinching yarn to form neck, and twist wire to secure. Let two long ends of excess wire extend from what will become back of neck.

3. To form skirt, draw scissors through each loop at bottom edge *B*, pull yarn taut, and cut.

4. To make arms, insert chenille stem from right to left between yarn strands below neck. Curve arms to meet in front. Pick up twelve yarn strands surrounding each arm, straighten, and wind tightly around chenille stem to conceal it. Tie short piece of yarn at each end of chenille stem to secure wound yarn. Trim excess yarn, leaving ½"-long yarn ends for hands.

5. To shape waist, twist 7" length of wire under arms as in Step 2, permitting excess wire to extend from back.

6. To make wings, cut two 12" lengths of lace. Glue ends together, forming two circles. Close each circle with glued seam at center, making two separate wing sections, each with one loop on each side. (See Illustration 2.) Crimp centers to resemble bows and secure with 1½" length of wire on each. Place wings together on angel's back, twisting wires from neck and waist around them tightly to secure. Cut off excess wire.

7. To make halo, twist end of tinsel stem into 1"-diameter circle, leaving excess stem attached. Bend stem at right angle to halo. (See Illustration 3.) Glue stem to center back of head with halo positioned over head.

8. To complete angel, glue ends of metallic-gold cord to back of head, forming a hanger. Make shoestring bow from 12" length of ¼"-wide mauve satin ribbon. Cut ribbon ends at an angle and glue bow at front of neck. Glue gift package between hands. Trim yarn strands even at bottom of skirt.

9. To make party favor or place-card holder, follow Steps 1–8 for ornament and proceed as follows.

Note: If making place-card holder, substitute place card for gift package in Step 8.

10. Cut thirty 9" lengths of yarn. Place cup, which will be base of angel, upside-down on a table. Completely conceal cup by gluing center of each yarn strand in center of bottom of cup, with ends of yarn radiating over entire cup like the spokes of a wheel. Run a beading of glue around outside edge of bottom of cup to hold yarn.

11. To complete favor or place-card holder, turn angel upside-down and separate strands of yarn that form skirt to radiate evenly from center. Glue bottom of cup to underside of angel, with all yarn strands radiating from center. Turn angel right-side up and trim yarn strands even at bottom of skirt.

Tatted Angels

> ### Tatting Abbreviations:
>
> **beg**—beginning
> **ch**—chain(s)
> **clr**—close ring
> **ds**—double stitch(es)
> **nxt**—next
> **p**—picot(s)
> **r**—ring
> **rep**—repeat(ing)
> **rw**—reverse work
> **sep**—separated
> **sk**—skip
> **tog**—together

White Angel
Materials:
14 yds. white Knit-Cro-Sheen **or** size 10 crochet thread for **each** angel
Tatting shuttle with hook for joining **or** shuttle **and** small crochet hook
Fabric or doily stiffener (**Note:** Designer used Aleene's fabric and doily stiffener.)
Clear acrylic spray
Small amount iridescent glitter
Thick white craft glue (**Note:** Designer used Aleene's designer tacky glue.)
Two 12" lengths 1/16"-wide ribbon in colors of your choice (for bows) (**Note:** Designer used mauve and light-blue ribbon for models.)
Plastic wrap

Finished size: 2¾" tall

Head, halo, and wings: Leaving ball of thread attached, wind 6 yds. of thread onto shuttle.

Work: R of 4ds, 8p sep by 2ds, 4ds, clr, rw. Body ch of 4ds, 8p sep by 2ds, 4ds, join to beg of r, do not cut and tie threads, continue ch to go around head for halo. Ch of 4ds, join to first p on head r, *2ds p 2ds, join to nxt p, rep from * around head, after joining to last p work 4ds, join to beg of head r, cut and tie threads.

Wings: Tie ball and shuttle threads together, join to first p on body ch, ch of 2ds, 8p sep by 2ds, 2ds, rw, r of 2ds, 3p

sep by 2ds, 2ds, clr, rw, ch of 2ds, 8p sep by 2ds, 2ds join to 3rd p on body ch, continue ch of 10ds, join to sixth p on body. Rep first wing, joining to last p and cutting and tying threads.

Skirt: First round: r of 2ds, p, 4ds, p, 2ds, clr, rw. *Ch of 2ds, 3p sep by 2ds, rw. R of 2ds, join to last p of last r, 4ds, p, 2ds, clr, rw, rep from * once more, rep ch once more, last r(4th), r of 2ds join to last p of last r, 4ds, join to first p of first r, 2ds, clr, rw, rep ch once more, cut and tie threads.

Second round: Tie threads together, work: r of 4ds, join to center p of any ch from first round, 4ds, clr, rw. *Ch of 2ds, 3p sep by 2ds, 2ds, rw, r of 4ds sk one p join to nxt (**Note:** You will be joining to middle p of one ch and to first and third p of nxt ch), 4ds, clr rw. Rep from * around, rep ch one last time and joining to beg of first r. Cut and tie threads. 6 r and ch.

Third round: Rep second round for a total of 9 r and ch.

Finishing:
1. Stiffen angel, following manufacturer's instructions. Shape head and wings flat. Shape skirt round by stuffing with plastic wrap. Let dry.
2. Pinch together top of skirt and glue to body ch ¼" below bottom of head.
3. Spray with acrylic sealer and sprinkle on glitter immediately.
4. Tie ribbon into small bow and glue to body under chin.

Blue Angel
Materials:
One 11-yd. (10m) spool medium (#16) braid from Kreinik Metallics, color: 094, star blue
Tatting shuttle with hook
Thick white craft glue
12" length 1/16"-wide white ribbon (for bow)

Finished size: 3" tall

Leaving ball attached, wind 5 yds. braid onto shuttle.

Head and body: Rep first r and body ch from *White Angel*.

Halo: Continue ch of 4ds, join to first p, *4ds, join to nxt p, rep from * around head to last p, 4ds, join to beg of head r, cut and tie threads.

Wings: Tie threads tog, join to first p on body ch, ch of 10ds, rw. R of 2ds p 2ds, join to second p on body ch, 2ds 2ds, clr, rw. Ch of 18ds, join to third p on body ch, continue ch of 9ds, join to sixth p of body ch. Rep first wing, working wing in r, ch 18ds, then r, then 10ds

33

ch, joining r to seventh p of body and ending by joining to eighth p. Cut and tie threads. Rep skirt from *White Angel*.

Finishing:
1. Secure all knots with a touch of glue.
2. Glue body and skirt together as for *White Angel*.
3. Tie ribbon into small bow and glue to body under chin.

Tiny Gold Angel
Materials:
9 yds. cable from Kreinik Metallics, color: 002P Gold
Tatting shuttle with hook
Thick white craft glue
12" length 1/16"-wide white ribbon (for bow)

Finished size: 2" tall

Leaving ball of thread attached, wind 4 yds. onto shuttle.
Work: Head, body, and halo as for *Blue Angel*.
Wings: Tie ball and shuttle threads together, join to first p on body, ch of 2ds, 4p sep by 2ds, 2ds, rw. R of 2ds p 2ds, join to 2nd p on body ch, 2ds p 2ds, clr, rw. Ch of 2ds, 10p sep by 2ds, 2ds, join to third p of body, continue ch of 10ds, join to sixth p of body. Second wing: Rep first wing, working in reverse, long ch of 2ds, 10p sep by 2ds, 2ds, then r joining to nxt-to-last p, then short ch of 2ds, 4p sep by 2ds, 2ds, joining to last p. Rep skirt from *White Angel*.

Finishing:
Refer to finishing instructions for *Blue Angel*.

Victorian-Look Ornaments

Crazy-Quilt Fans
Materials:
21" x 36" x 1½"-thick sheet STYROFOAM brand plastic foam (**Note:** Sixteen ornaments can be made from this size sheet.)
Small scraps velvet, cotton, satin, moiré taffeta, lamé, and assorted bridal fabrics in coordinating colors of your choice (**Note:** Designer used black, purple, lavender, teal green, and light green fabrics.)
5" square complementary fabric for **each** ornament (for backing)
15¾" length ⅜"-wide black grosgrain ribbon for **each** ornament
Assorted scraps lace trim, ribbon, braided trim, rickrack, rattail cord, and sequin trim

Assorted sequins, beads, faux pearls, satin roses or bows, and motifs cut from lace trim
6" length ⅛"-wide black satin ribbon for **each** ornament (for hangers)
Serrated steak knife **or** #5 artist's painting knife (**Note:** Artist's painting knife has a point and two blade surfaces that are handy for tucking the small seams.)
Pin board (**Note:** Designer used an empty fabric reel from a local fabric store.)
Template plastic **or** cardboard

Fine-line permanent marker
Aleene's Thick Designer Tacky Glue™
Tracing paper and pencil
Ruler   Straight pins
Toothpicks
Scissors

1. Make fan-shape pattern, using template plastic or cardboard and following pattern given.
2. Using tracing paper and pencil, trace pattern three times. Mark all design lines and number pattern pieces as indicated on pattern.

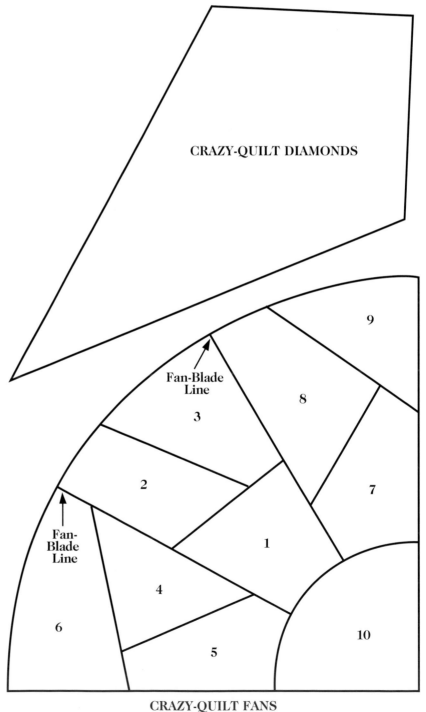

CRAZY-QUILT DIAMONDS

CRAZY-QUILT FANS

3. Using serrated steak knife and a sawing motion, cut a 4¼" square from Styrofoam® for **each** ornament.

4. Following fan-shape pattern from Step 1, mark top curve of fan shape on Styrofoam® square, using permanent marker. Carefully cut curve using serrated steak knife. Gently "sand" rough edges with a scrap of Styrofoam®.

5. Pin one tracing-paper pattern (master pattern) to fabric reel or other pin board. Cut second tracing-paper pattern on bottom curve and two fan-blade lines. Use these pieces to mark bottom curve and two fan-blade lines on Styrofoam® fans, using permanent marker. (**Note:** Use a permanent marker. **Do not** use a water-based ink marker since ink may bleed through fabric when trims are glued in place.) Cut apart the third tracing-paper pattern along all design lines. Referring to master pattern, use these pieces to mark patchwork design lines on Styrofoam® fan. (**Note:** You will also use these pieces to cut out fabrics. After marking, pin pattern pieces in place atop master pattern to keep track of them.)

6. Score all design lines on Styrofoam® fan, using sharp pencil.

7. Pin pattern pieces right-side up atop right side of fabric scraps. (**Note:** For delicate fabrics, you may wish to hold pattern in place with fingers.) Trace around pattern pieces and cut out, adding ¼" seam allowance to all sides.

8. Working on a flat surface, center fabric piece 1 atop scored design. Position serrated steak knife or artist's painting knife over fabric and scored lines. Push seam allowances into Styrofoam®, using tip of knife. Repeat for pieces 2–10.

9. Glue outside seam allowances to edge of fan, mitering corners for a neat appearance.

10. Place fan atop wrong side of backing fabric. Trace around fan. Cut out, adding ¼" seam allowance to all sides. Clip top curve at ½" intervals to traced line. Place fabric on back of fan and glue seam allowances to edge of fan.

11. Glue ⅜"-wide black grosgrain ribbon around edge of ornament, beginning and ending at bottom point of fan.

12. Cut trims to fit seam lines and glue in place as desired, beginning with shorter lines first and referring to photo on page **16**. Glue trim to fan-blade lines. Glue trim to top and bottom curves.

Note: For a neat look, use toothpick to spread fine line of glue in seams.

13. Glue additional decorations in place as desired, referring to photo for ideas.

14. Bring ends of 6" length ⅛"-wide ribbon together and tie a knot in ribbon ends to form hanging loop. Glue hanger to back of ornament, aligning with left-hand fan-blade line.

Crazy-Quilt Diamonds
Materials:
4" x 7" scrap 1"-thick STYROFOAM brand plastic foam sheet for **each** ornament

Assorted fabric scraps in complementary colors of your choice (**Note:** Designer used burgundy, purple, teal green, mauve, and black.)

4" x 7" scrap complementary fabric for **each** ornament (for backing)

15" length 1"-wide purple grosgrain ribbon for **each** ornament

1 yd. ⅜"-wide picot-edged burgundy satin ribbon for **each** ornament

1 mauve fabric rose for **each** ornament

7" length metallic-gold cord for **each** ornament (for hanger)

Assorted lace and braid trims, cord, beads, stones, fabric roses and bows of your choice

White craft glue

Utility blade

1" putty knife

Butter knife

Straight pins

Fine-line permanent marker

Tracing paper and pencil

1. Place pattern atop Styrofoam® sheet and trace around pattern. Cut out diamond shape from Styrofoam®, using utility blade.

2. Draw crazy-quilt pattern on front of diamond shape as desired, using fine-line permanent marker and referring to photo on page **16**.

3. Place tracing paper atop diamond shape and trace crazy-quilt pattern. Cut crazy-quilt pieces apart, forming pattern pieces. Pin pattern pieces right-side up atop right side of fabric scraps and trace around pieces. Cut out fabric pieces, cutting pieces ⅜" larger all around than marked.

Note: Place fabric pieces atop diamond as you prepare pieces, checking to be sure you are creating a pleasing arrangement of color and texture.

4. Place one fabric piece atop diamond. Position knife over fabric and marked lines. Push seam allowances into diamond along marked lines, using tip of knife. Repeat for remaining pieces until ornament front is

covered. Glue seam allowances along edges of diamond to side edges of diamond.

5. Place pattern right-side up atop right side of backing fabric and trace lightly around pattern. Cut out, leaving a ⅜" seam allowance around all edges. Glue fabric to back of ornament. Glue seam allowances along edges of diamond to side edges of diamond.

6. Cut trims to fit seam lines; glue in place as desired, beginning with shorter lines first and referring to photo. Glue on additional trims as desired, referring to photo.

7. Cover sides of ornament by gluing on 1"-wide purple ribbon, beginning and ending at bottom point of diamond.

8. Bring ends of 7" length of metallic-gold cord together and tie a knot in thread ends to form hanging loop. Pin hanger to top center of ornament.

9. Tie ⅜"-wide burgundy ribbon into a multi-looped bow. Pin and then glue to top center of ornament. Glue fabric rose atop center of bow.

Hot Air Balloon Ornaments
Materials:
One 3½" STYROFOAM brand plastic foam ball

1 small basket (approximately 1⅜" in diameter) with handles removed

Two–four ⅛-yd. 44/45"-wide pieces of coordinating fabrics in colors of your choice (**Note:** Designer used combinations of teal green, light green, purple, and lavender fabrics.)

One 31½" length Pearls by the Yard, metallic silver baby rickrack, **or** other trim of your choice

11" length lace, ribbon, sequins, **or** other trim of your choice

27" length ⅛"-wide satin ribbon **or** other trim in complementary colors (for hanger and basket strings)

8" lengths ⅛"-wide ribbon in complementary colors (for trimming baskets)

Acrylic mirrors, tiny bows, rhinestones, sequins, beads, **or** other assorted trims of your choice

#5 artist's painting knife **or** serrated steak knife (**Note:** Artist's painting knife has a point and two blade surfaces that are handy for tucking the small seams.)

3" square heavy tracing paper **or** typing paper (for pattern)

Fine-line permanent marker

Aleene's Thick Designer Tacky Glue™

Silver spray paint (**Note:** Designer

used Accent® Essential Metallics, color: #154 Silver.)
One 35" length string
One 14" length string
Small piece aluminum foil
3 glass-head pins
2 sequin pins
1 silver ring bead
Three tiny packages
Sharp pencil
Toothpicks
Scissors Straight pins

Note: Materials listed will make one *Hot Air Balloon Ornament.*

1. Spray baskets inside and out, using silver spray paint and following manufacturer's instructions. Let dry.
2. Place glass-head pins in north and south poles of 3½" Styrofoam® ball. Tie one end of 35" length of string to one pin. Wrap string around ball and two pins, dividing ball in half, and continue wrapping string around ball two more times, dividing ball into sixths. Anchor end of string to pin. Place third pin at mid-circumference point. Tie 14" length of string to this pin. Wrap string around ball and pin, dividing ball in half horizontally. Anchor end of string around pin. Carefully arrange strings so that you have twelve equal sections.
3. Mark ball along lines of strings, using fine-line permanent marker. Remove strings. Remove pins.
4. Place tracing paper atop one section and trace. Cut out. This is your pattern for cutting fabrics.
5. Score marked lines of ball, using sharp pencil.
6. Pin pattern right-side up atop right side of fabric and cut out, adding a ¼" seam allowance on all sides. Cut out twelve fabric sections for **each** ornament.
7. Center one fabric section atop scored section on top half of ball. Place tip of artist's painting knife or serrated knife on fabric atop scored lines and push seam allowance into scored lines. Repeat this tucking process, working around ball until top half is covered with fabric. Repeat for bottom half of ball.
8. Cut to fit and glue Pearls by the Yard, rickrack, or cord atop vertical seams from north to south poles.
9. Cut four 5" lengths from ⅛"-wide ribbon or other trim. Glue one end of each ribbon to mid-circumference point of ball, spacing evenly around ball. Glue opposite end of each length of ribbon to inside of small basket at front, back, and both sides. (**Note:** By gluing

ribbon lengths to ball first, it will be easy to make any necessary adjustments at opposite end to make basket hang level before gluing ribbon in place.)
10. Cut to fit and glue lace, ribbon, or a combination of trims of your choice at mid-circumference of ball.
11. Decorate balloons with acrylic mirrors, tiny bows, pearls, rhinestones, or other trims of your choice, referring to photo on page **16** for placement and ideas.
12. Glue a scrunched ball of aluminum foil in bottom of basket. Glue three tiny packages in basket so that they extend above edge of basket.
13. To make hanger, cut 7" length of ⅛"-wide ribbon or other trim and knot ends together. Separate cut ends and glue to top center of ball, placing a sequin pin through each end and into ball. Slip ring bead over loop and glue to top center of ball.

Foyer Tree

Note: For these projects, a marbling materials list and instructions have been given. Materials and instructions for projects have been listed separately.

Materials for marbling:
2 qts. Sta-Flo® liquid starch
Shallow, disposable pan, at least 10" x 12"
Old newspapers
Paper towels
Broom straw, thin wire, **or** hair pick
DecoArt Americana acrylic paints, colors: Berry Red, Viridian Green, Ultra Blue Deep, Crystal Green, Glorious Gold Metallic, Ice Blue
Plastic **or** paper cup for **each** color
Small paintbrush for **each** color
White drawing paper **or** construction paper (**Note:** 80 lb. paper works best, but paper heavier than typing paper will work.)
Press cloth
Spoon
Pencil
Iron

General instructions for marbling:
1. Shake starch very well and pour into pan. Starch should be about 1½" deep in pan. Let sit until bubbles disperse. Help them along by gently "dragging" the edge of a piece of newspaper over the surface, pulling bubbles to the side.
2. Place a small amount (approximately ½ tsp.) of paint in a cup. Add drops of water until paint is the consistency of cream. Mix with paintbrush. Mix each color in a separate cup.

3. Load paintbrush with paint and gently shake or tap it over the starch. Notice how some colors spread and push other colors around. Use broom straw, thin wire, or hair pick to "comb" color droplets into a design. Do not comb too much, or design will look muddy. When design is pleasing to you, pick up a sheet of paper, holding it at both ends. Lower paper onto surface of starch, touching the middle first and letting paper down from the center out.
Note: Just laying the paper down would work, but air bubbles trapped between paper and starch would leave white spots.
4. Pull paper off starch, holding one end. Let starch drip back into pan. Hold paper under gentle stream of cool water to wash off excess starch, then place marbled paper on newspaper to dry. Blot paper lightly with paper towels to remove excess starch and water. Let dry.
Note: Drag surface of the starch after each marbling to clean off leftover paint. Each design will be different. After approximately five designs are marbled, stir starch with a spoon to keep it thick. If designs begin to look dull or muddy, dispose of starch and refill with new starch.
5. When papers are dry, iron backs to flatten. Iron fronts, covering with press cloth to keep paint off iron.

Materials:
1 sheet 140 lb. white watercolor paper
1 yd. Pellon® Wonder-Under® Transfer Web
1 small bottle R & R fine crystalescent glitter
Yarn Tree Designs needlework cards (and envelopes): one red with rectangular window, one ivory with oval window
8" length silver thread (for **each** ornament hanger)
Aleene's Thin-Bodied Glue
¼" and ⅛" hole punch
1 sheet 90 lb. ivory drawing paper **or** pastel paper
Small paintbrush
Scissors

Note: Please read all instructions carefully before beginning. Materials listed will make at least twelve heart ornaments, three bookmarks, three cards, and two window cards.

Ornaments
1. Trace large hearts onto watercolor paper and cut out. Trace same number

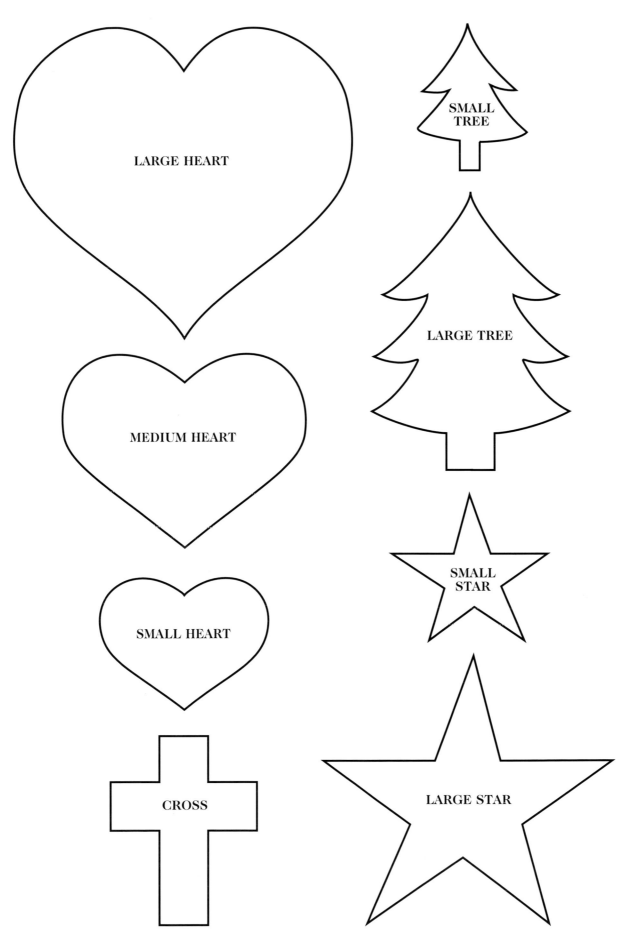

LARGE HEART

SMALL
TREE

MEDIUM HEART

LARGE TREE

SMALL HEART

SMALL
STAR

CROSS

LARGE STAR

PATTERNS FOR FOYER TREE PROJECTS

of medium hearts onto paper side of Wonder-Under®. Fuse to back side of marbled paper, following manufacturer's instructions for fusing, and cut out.

2. Fuse each marbled heart in center of large heart. Paint surface with thin-bodied glue and sprinkle on glitter. Let dry.

3. Punch ⅛" hole at top center of heart. Insert 8" length of silver thread through hole and tie a knot in thread ends to form hanger.

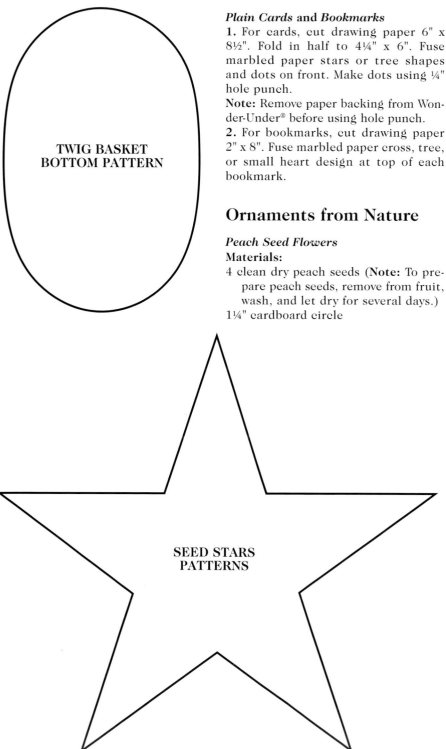

TWIG BASKET BOTTOM PATTERN

SEED STARS PATTERNS

ORNAMENTS FROM NATURE PATTERNS

Needlework Window Cards
1. For red card, glue white watercolor paper behind window. Trace tree onto paper side of Wonder-Under®, fuse to marbled paper, and cut out. Fuse tree shape to watercolor paper.

2. For ivory card with marbled oval, cut rectangle from marbled paper to fit behind window, and glue in place.

Option: Add odd shapes of marbled scraps to envelope.

Plain Cards and *Bookmarks*
1. For cards, cut drawing paper 6" x 8½". Fold in half to 4¼" x 6". Fuse marbled paper stars or tree shapes and dots on front. Make dots using ¼" hole punch.

Note: Remove paper backing from Wonder-Under® before using hole punch.

2. For bookmarks, cut drawing paper 2" x 8". Fuse marbled paper cross, tree, or small heart design at top of each bookmark.

Ornaments from Nature

Peach Seed Flowers
Materials:
4 clean dry peach seeds (**Note:** To prepare peach seeds, remove from fruit, wash, and let dry for several days.)
1¼" cardboard circle

Dried globe amaranth
8" length metallic-gold thread
Aleene's Thick Designer Tacky Glue™
Scissors

Note: Materials listed will make one *Peach Seed Flower.*

1. Apply glue to large end of one peach seed and press seed atop cardboard circle. Glue second seed to cardboard opposite first seed. Repeat to glue two remaining seeds to cardboard. Let dry.

2. Glue dried globe amaranth in center of peach seeds. Let dry.

3. Bring thread ends together and tie in a knot to form hanger. Glue knotted end to back of one peach seed to complete.

Watermelon Seed Wreaths
Materials:
120 clean dry watermelon seeds
4" cardboard ring with 3" circle cut out of center
Spray paint, color: gold metallic
8" length mauve raffia
7" length metallic-gold thread
Aleene's Thick Designer Tacky Glue™
Scissors

Note: Materials listed will make one *Watermelon Seed Wreath.*

1. Apply even coat of glue over one-fourth of cardboard ring. Press two rows of seeds into glue along inner and outer edges of cardboard, extending larger ends of seeds ¼" over edges of cardboard. Glue another row of seeds along center of ring where first two rows meet. Repeat to cover remainder of ring with seeds. Let dry.

2. Spray front and back of wreath with gold-metallic paint. Let dry.

3. Loop thread around wreath and tie in a knot around wreath to secure. Bring thread ends together and tie in a knot to form hanger.

4. Tie raffia into a bow and glue to bottom, center of wreath.

Pinecone Flowers
Materials:
Pinecones in sizes of your choice
Dried yarrow
Aleene's Thick Designer Tacky Glue™
8" length metallic-gold thread
Small hand saw

1. For **each** flower, saw 1½" off large end of pinecone. Remove several burs from bottom of another pinecone and glue to cut center of pinecone slice. Let dry.

2. Glue dried yarrow to center of pinecone slice. Work gold thread around several burs on pinecone flower, and bring thread ends together and tie in a knot to form hanger.

Flower Wreath
Materials:
3" grapevine wreath
15 dried pink globe amaranth blossoms
7" length metallic-gold thread
Aleene's Thick Designer Tacky Glue™

1. Loop thread around top of wreath and tie in a knot around wreath to secure. Bring thread ends together and tie in a knot to form hanger.
2. Glue globe amaranth blossoms to front of wreath. Let dry.

Gilded Walnuts
Materials:
Walnut
7" length metallic-gold thread
Spray paint, color: gold metallic
Aleene's Thick Designer Tacky Glue™
Scissors

Note: Materials listed will make one *Gilded Walnut.*

1. Bring thread ends together and tie in a knot to form hanger. Glue knotted end to top of walnut. Let dry.
2. Spray walnut with gold-metallic paint. Let dry.

Floral Bouquets
Materials:
Six 8"-long stems dried mini-gyp
3 stems pink globe amaranth
Stem of dried hydrangea
Fabric-covered spool wire
12" length mauve raffia

Note: Materials listed will make one *Floral Bouquet.*

1. Make bouquet with mini-gyp stems. Add globe amaranth and dried hydrangea to bouquet. Wrap stems together to secure, using wire.
2. Wrap raffia around stems to cover wire; tie raffia into a bow.

Popcorn Balls
Materials:
1½ cups stale, popped popcorn
3" STYROFOAM brand plastic foam ball
2" length white, fabric-covered stem wire
7" length metallic-gold thread
Aleene's Thick Designer Tacky Glue™
Clear acrylic spray
Scissors

Note: Materials listed will make one *Popcorn Ball.*

1. Bend wire into a "U" shape. Apply glue to ends and insert ends into ball.
2. Glue pieces of popcorn to ball one at a time, continuing until ball is covered. Let dry.
3. Spray ball with clear acrylic spray. Let dry.
4. Insert thread through wire loop, bring thread ends together, and tie in a knot to form hanger.

Indian Corn Balls
Materials:
1 ear Indian corn
2" STYROFOAM brand plastic foam ball
2" length white, fabric-covered stem wire
7" length metallic-gold thread
8" length mauve raffia
Spray paint, color: gold metallic
Aleene's Thick Designer Tacky Glue™
Clear acrylic spray
Scissors
Paring knife

Note: One ear of corn will cover two balls.

1. Bend wire into a "U" shape. Apply glue to ends and insert ends into ball.
2. Spray ball with gold-metallic paint. Let dry.
3. Cut kernels off car of corn, using paring knife. Glue kernels to ball one at a time, continuing until ball is covered. Let dry.
4. Spray ball with clear acrylic spray. Let dry.
5. Insert thread through wire loop, bring thread ends together, and tie in a knot to form hanger. Tie raffia into a bow and glue to top of ball in front of wire.

Seed Stars
Materials:
150–200 dry cantaloupe seeds
4½" square cardboard
Acrylic paint, color: metallic gold
Small paintbrush
7" length metallic-gold thread
Aleene's Thick Designer Tacky Glue™
Tracing paper
Pencil
Scissors

Note: Materials listed will make one *Seed Star.*

1. Trace around star pattern and cut out. Place pattern atop cardboard and trace around pattern. Cut out star shape from cardboard, using scissors.
2. Paint back of star with gold-metallic paint. Let dry.
3. Apply even coat of glue over one point of star. Press on seeds to cover point, beginning at tip and placing seeds close together. Repeat for remaining star points.
4. Spread glue atop center of star. Press on seeds to form a circle, overlapping edges of seeds at base of each point and continuing to fill in center.
5. Bring thread ends together and tie in a knot to form hanger. Glue knotted end to back of one point of star to complete.

Twig Baskets
Materials:
⅛"–¼" diameter green twigs with leaves removed, cut into 2½" pieces and one 12" piece (for handle) (**Note:** Designer used privet-hedge twigs.)
Nuts and small pinecones of your choice
2" x 9" piece lightweight cardboard (for sides of basket)
2½" x 3½" piece lightweight cardboard (for bottom of basket)
2" x 3¼" scrap STYROFOAM brand plastic foam
30" length natural raffia
7" length metallic-gold thread
Tracing paper and pencil
Scissors
Hot glue gun and glue sticks

1. Trace around pattern for bottom of basket and cut out. Place pattern atop cardboard and trace around pattern. Cut out shape from 2½" x 3½" piece lightweight cardboard, using scissors. Apply hot glue ¼" from edge along one long edge and one short edge of cardboard for sides of basket. Place edge of liner bottom piece in glue and wrap sides around it, overlapping ends. Hold in place until glue sets.
2. Glue ends of handle twig to opposite sides of cardboard basket liner, centering on outside of sides. Hold in place until glue sets. Glue 2½" twig pieces around basket to cover, beginning at one side of handle.
3. Glue raffia around top and bottom edges of basket, referring to photo on page **20** for placement. Tie a small raffia bow and glue at top, center of basket, referring to photo for placement.
4. Cut Styrofoam® to fit inside basket and glue in place. Fill basket with nuts and pinecones as desired, gluing to secure.
5. Insert thread through loop formed by basket handle, bring thread ends together, and tie in a knot to form hanger.

FESTIVE TABLES

The age-old tradition of Christmas dinner can bring family members together for a joyous celebration of the season like no other holiday custom. Because delicious, home-cooked meals are at the very heart of most yuletide gatherings, we think the table provides an ideal place to create focal points that will leave everyone who joins you at the dinner table "oohing" and "aahing" over the decorations as much as the meal! In this chapter, we feature a variety of place mats and centerpieces for holiday tables of all kinds; from quick-and-easy candy canes, to a decorative pineapple, to elegant candles and fruit, to contemporary arches and snowflakes. Whether you prefer traditional trimmings or those with a touch of lighthearted charm, you're certain to find the perfect tabletop decor for your annual festivities.

Tabletop Decor

We have found, over the years, that while some holiday decorating ideas remain basically the same, certain areas offer endless possibilities for creating a new look each year. Our favorite "quick changes" are centerpieces and table "linens" used on the informal kitchen table and the more formal dining-room table. Consider how tabletop arrangements, both those that are made from fresh greenery and those that are assembled from inanimate materials, open up a multitude of ideas. Create your linens to match, or let them be the inspiration for your tabletop decor.

Above and right—We all like the lovely **Candy-Stripe Place Mat Set,** *right. The red-and-white striped borders and bright green binding make a cheery backdrop for holiday china. Simple to make, yet eye-catching, the* **Candy-Cane Centerpiece,** *above, is destined to become a Christmas classic. Peppermint sticks surround a can and are tied with a jaunty red bow, making a spirited container for holiday-inspired floral arrangements. To complete your holiday dinner table, create our felt stockings, which serve as charming holders for napkins and silverware. Instructions begin on page 50.*

The **Fruit Tree** is wrapped with an evergreen garland to cover the foundation, which is, believe it or not, a tomato cage. Yes, the very kind you can buy in any nursery for use in your vegetable garden! Added to that is an assortment of plastic fruit, including apples, peaches, pears, oranges, strawberries, grapes, and plums. Place this bountiful tree on a hall table, perhaps with a bowl of fruit and a fruit-motif candelabra, to greet guests as they enter your home. Instructions are on page 52.

For a Victorian look, the **Ivy and Rose Tree** *features garlands of ivy twined around a tomato-cage base. This elegant tree is adorned with mauve ribbon and silk roses and rosebuds in shades of off-white, pink, mauve, and maroon. You can choose your own colors of floral decoration, but we think this combination is fresh and romantic—fabulous for a guest room or a formal sitting room. Instructions are on page 52.*

Above—The pineapple has long been considered a symbol of hospitality, and we think this **Pineapple Centerpiece** will welcome your holiday dinner guests quite effectively. Start with a fresh, unripened pineapple; then spray-paint it gold; add red acrylic stones and red Christmas balls; and arrange fresh greenery around the pineapple on a plate. Instructions are on page 52.

Right—The **Candles and Fruit Centerpiece** will complement a formal dining table perfectly. The candlelight from five red tapers will glisten off the glitter-coated fruit and greenery as you and your family members or guests enjoy a yuletide feast. Instructions are on page 52.

*Above—Add a touch of country charm to your holiday decorating with a **Ragtag Calico Tree.** The tree shown here uses traditional holiday colors, but if you prefer, you can create your own decorative using nontraditional favorites of your own. By using a variety of fabric colors that match the colors used in your home, you can also transform this piece into a year-round table topper that is certain to catch the eye of everyone who visits! Instructions are on page 53.*

Above and left—Dramatic black arches, above, form a showcase for hand-cut snowflakes. Reindeer napkin holders complete the look for a modern approach to holiday decorating. We think these pieces will make a wonderful backdrop for a New Year's Eve party. For a more traditional look and for use during the Christmas season, use red, green, or Christmas-plaid fabric and hang your favorite ornaments from the arches. Instructions begin on page 53.

Candy-Stripe Place Mat Set

Materials:
1½ yds. 44/45"-wide white candy-cane-print fabric
1½ yds. 44/45"-wide red candy-cane-print fabric
1½ yds. solid red fabric (for backing)
2 pkgs. Coats Wide Bias Tape, color: 177 Kerry Green
3 pkgs. Coats Extra-Wide Double-Fold Bias Tape, color: 177 Kerry Green
1 spool **each** Coats Dual Duty Plus thread, colors: White, Kerry Green, Atom Red
1 spool Coats clear monofilament
2 yds. Pellon® Thermolam Plus Fleece
Straight pins
Scissors
Iron
Sewing machine

Note: Use ¼" seam allowances throughout. Yardage given will make four place mats and napkins.

1. Cut four 12" squares and six 2½" x 20" strips from white print fabric.
2. Cut four 14" squares and six 2½" x 20" strips from red print fabric.
3. Sew one red strip and one white strip together lengthwise. Make six sets of these strips. Cut strips at a 45-degree angle every 2½" to make diagonal striped sections for sides of place mats. (See Illustration A.) Sew all sections together to make one long strip. Cut strip into eight 12"-long strips. Set aside.
Note: There will be fabric leftover after cutting 12"-long strips.
4. Cut eight 12"-long strips of single-fold bias tape. Sew one strip to each

side of white 12" square. (See Illustration B.) Sew one candy-stripe strip to each bias-tape strip. Press seams toward center.
5. Cut four 14" x 20" rectangles **each** from red solid fabric (for backing) and fleece. Layer backing fabric right-side down, fleece, and place-mat top right-side up atop a flat surface. Pin or baste layers together.
6. Load machine with clear monofilament on top and white thread in bobbin. Machine-quilt along all seam lines, and diagonally in one direction in white place-mat center. Space quilting 1" apart in center section. (See Illustration C.)
Note: Loosening upper tension slightly may be helpful when working with monofilament.
7. Trim edges of backing and fleece even with place-mat top and bind with double-fold bias tape, using green thread.
8. Hem napkins with a ⅛" double hem. Press.

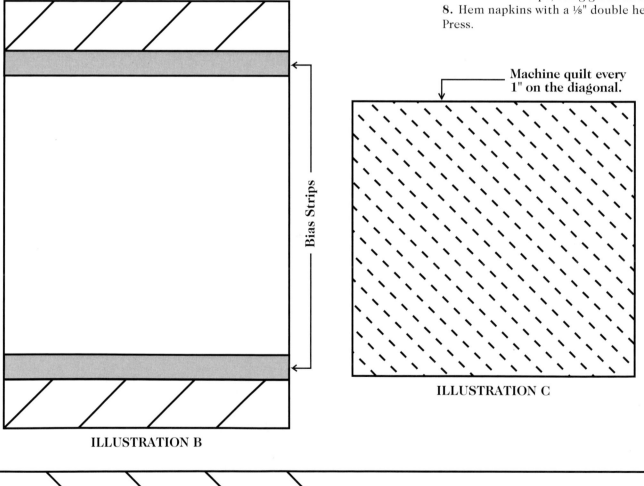

ILLUSTRATION B

ILLUSTRATION C

Machine quilt every 1" on the diagonal.

Bias Strips

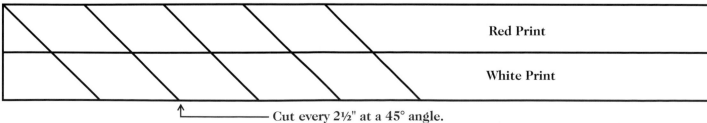

Red Print

White Print

Cut every 2½" at a 45° angle.
ILLUSTRATION A

Candy-Cane Centerpiece

Materials:

28-oz. aluminum can, empty, washed,
  with label removed
Thirty-six 5½"-long candy canes with
  curved ends
1 yd. ⅞"-wide red taffeta floral ribbon
Potted poinsettia **or** your choice of
  silk or real flowers and greenery
Hot glue gun and glue sticks

1. Apply glue to can in straight line
from top to bottom and press cane
into glue, placing curved end at top.
Repeat with remaining candy canes
until can is covered. Let dry.
2. Place ribbon around canes near top
of can and tie ribbon into a bow.
3. Place potted poinsettia inside can.
Option: Fill can with silk or real flowers and greenery.

Napkin and Silverware Holders

Materials:

9" x 12" piece red felt
1½" x 9" piece white felt
16" square red-and-white checked ging-
  ham
Aleene's Original All-Purpose Tacky Glue
Hand-sewing needle
Red embroidery thread
Red sewing thread
Tracing paper and pencil
Straight pins
Scissors
Sewing machine

OUTLINE STITCH

Note: Materials listed will make one
Napkin and Silverware Holder.

Silverware Holder
1. Cut out stocking pattern. Pin pattern atop red felt and trace around
pattern twice to make stocking front
and back. Remove pattern. Cut out
stocking pieces.
2. Pin stocking pieces together and
machine sew together around perimeter ⅛" in from edge, leaving top of
stocking open.
3. Cut white felt in half to make two
1½" x 4½" pieces. Print or write name
lightly on center of one piece of felt,

using pencil. Thread needle with three
strands red embroidery thread and
embroider name, using outline stitch.
4. Glue remaining piece white felt to
back of embroidered piece to form cuff.
Let dry. Glue cuff to top of stocking,
extending sides of cuff ⅛" on each side
at top of stocking.

Napkin
1. Machine sew ⅝" in from edge
around perimeter of 16" square of
gingham, using small stitches. Fringe
to stitching.
2. Fold napkin and insert into stocking and then insert silverware.

**NAPKIN AND SILVERWARE
HOLDERS STOCKING PATTERN**

Fruit Tree

Materials:
38"–40"-tall tomato cage
18' silk evergreen garland (with branches)
5 holly-berry picks (with approximately 30 berries per pick)
Assorted plastic fruits (**Note:** Designer used 7 clusters of grapes, 5 peaches, 7 apples, 5 pears, 5 plums, 3 clusters of strawberries, and 3 tangerines.)
Small bunch German statice
24-gauge wire
Measuring tape
Wire cutters
Ice pick
Hot glue gun and glue sticks

1. Wire three long prongs of tomato cage together to form top of tree.
2. Measure perimeter of **each** horizontal ring of tomato cage and cut piece of garland to correspond with **each** measurement. Attach garland lengths to outside of rings in several places, using 4" lengths of wire. Measure lengths of the three vertical, metal supports of tomato cage. Cut piece of garland to fit **each** support; wire in place. Arrange branches to cover exposed metal areas.
Note: If necessary, cut small pieces of garland; glue where needed to fill in.
3. Pierce two holes in back side of **each** piece of fruit, **except** clusters of strawberries and grapes, using ice pick. Cut a 6" length of wire for **each** piece of pierced fruit. Thread wire end into one hole and out remaining hole in **each** piece of fruit and then attach fruit securely to tree, twisting wire ends together. Wrap wire around stems of clusters of strawberries and grapes; wire to tree.
4. Break off small pieces of statice; glue to greenery. Glue holly berries to tree in clusters of three berries each, placing as desired.

Ivy and Rose Tree

Materials:
38"–40"-tall tomato cage
20' silk ivy garland
13 yds. 1¼"-wide mauve ribbon
Silk roses and rosebuds (**Note:** Designer used 26 off-white, 52 pink, 24 mauve, and 28 maroon.)
4 mauve chenille stems
Spray paint, color: green
24-gauge wire
Wire cutters

Hot glue gun and glue sticks
Acrylic paint, color: metallic gold (optional)
½" paintbrush (optional)

1. Wire three long prongs of tomato cage together to form top of tree. Spray tomato cage with green paint and let dry.
2. Measure perimeter of **each** horizontal ring of tomato cage and cut lengths of ivy garland to correspond with measurements. Attach garland lengths to outside of rings in several places, using 2½" lengths of wire. Measure lengths of the three vertical, metal supports of tomato cage. Cut piece of garland to fit **each** support and wire in place.
3. Cut four 2½-yard lengths from ribbon. Make a multi-loop bow with **each** length of ribbon and secure center with chenille stem. Center three of the four bows on middle ring and glue in place, referring to photo on page **45** for placement. Set fourth bow aside.
4. Cut three 1-yard lengths of ribbon and wire to top of tree. Bring ribbon streamers down behind rings, keeping ribbon straight and gluing to first ring and behind bow. Wire fourth bow to top of tree atop ribbon streamers.
5. Wire roses and rosebuds to tree, referring to photo for placement. (**Note:** Most flowers on bottom ring are glued on.) If necessary, cut off ivy leaves; glue to fill in areas where wire is exposed or tree appears too open.
6. Paint random leaves with gold paint, if desired.

Pineapple Centerpiece

Materials:
Fresh pineapple
9mm red acrylic stones (**Note:** Designer used 120 acrylic stones. Number of stones needed will vary, depending on size of pineapple.)
Twenty ½"-diameter red Christmas balls
Spray paint, color: gold
Large round serving plate
Fresh evergreen sprigs
Low-temperature glue gun and glue sticks

Note: This centerpiece is perishable. For longest use, purchase a green (not yet ripe) pineapple, which will last several days.

1. Spray pineapple evenly with gold spray paint. Let dry.
2. Glue an acrylic stone to center of each pineapple section. Glue balls between leaves. Let dry.
3. Center pineapple atop serving plate. Arrange evergreen sprigs around pineapple as desired.

Candles and Fruit Centerpiece

Materials:
12" x 2"-thick STYROFOAM brand plastic foam ring
Assorted plastic fruits (**Note:** Designer used 2 grapes, 4 apples, 5 pears, 2 oranges, 2 lemons, and 3 nectarines.)
120 pieces 3"-long silk greenery
32 large silk ivy leaves
2 yds. 1¼"-wide green ribbon
Five 12"-tall red candles
9" x 24" piece stiff cardboard
Clear glitter
Small paintbrush
Craft glue (for glitter)
Pencil
Scissors
Toothpicks
Low-temperature glue gun and glue sticks

1. Spread thin coat of craft glue over top or bottom third of each piece of fruit and individual grapes, using paintbrush. Sprinkle on glitter. Let glue dry and then gently shake off excess glitter. (**Note:** Complete one piece of fruit at a time.) Repeat for leaves, applying glue along edges. Set aside.
2. To make base, cut ring in half, and insert toothpicks into one end of one piece. Apply glue to one end of remaining half and press ends together to form an "S." (**Note:** Toothpicks will help hold pieces together while glue sets.) Let dry. Place Styrofoam® shape atop cardboard and trace around edges. Cut shape from cardboard and glue to bottom of Styrofoam® shape.
3. Glue ribbon around lower edge of base sides and ends.
4. Insert two rows of greenery into base, directly above top edge of ribbon. Glue candles into top of base, spacing evenly. Glue clusters of grapes to each end and six fruits to each side of base. Then glue a piece of fruit between each candle.
5. Glue ivy leaves and remaining pieces of greenery randomly, as desired.

Ragtag Calico Tree

Materials:

3'-long ¾" wooden dowel (for trunk)

Three 3'-long ⅜" wooden dowels (for branches)

5" x 6" x 1½"-thick wood scrap (for base)

1 yd. 44/45"-wide green calico

¼ yd. 44/45"-wide red calico

Polyester filling **or** fabric scraps (for stuffing)

Red thread

Red yarn **or** ribbon (for ornament hangers)

Large hand-sewing needle

Green paint to match calico

Paintbrush

Tacky white glue

Scissors

Sewing machine

Saw

Drill with ¾" and ⅜" bits

1. Paint wood base. Let dry.
2. Tear green calico into 45 strips, each 1" x 32".
3. Drill six holes for the ⅜" dowels (branches) in the ¾" dowel (tree trunk). For placement of holes, measure down from top of trunk and drill one hole 6" down, another 13" down, and another 21" down. Turn tree a quarter turn and drill holes perpendicular to and ¼" below first set of holes. Be sure ⅜" dowels will fit into holes easily, as they may break if forced. Drill ¾" hole approximately 1" deep in center of base, and insert trunk.
4. Cut ⅜" dowels into branch lengths: two 22½" long, two 16½" long, and two 10½" long. Insert branches into trunk with shortest on top, longest on bottom.

5. Wrap trunk and branches with calico strips as needed to cover, securing ends with glue. Cut remaining strips into 8" lengths. Attach to tree branches with lark's-head knot. (See illustration.) Twist fabric knots around branches in a random pattern. Glue end knot on each branch to secure.
6. Cut out heart ornament pattern and pin to double thickness of red calico, folded with right sides of fabric together. Cut out number of ornaments desired. Sew around each heart, using a ⅝" seam allowance and leaving an opening for turning. Trim seam allowance, turn, and stuff lightly. Whipstitch opening closed. With large, sharp needle, thread yarn or ribbon through each ornament, and tie a knot in thread ends to form hanger.

Black and White Table Toppers

Snowflakes
Materials:

5" x 24" piece 140 lb. watercolor paper **or** 3 sheets heavy typing paper

Tracing paper and pencil

7" length silver thread for **each** ornament (for hanger)

Hand-sewing needle

Scissors

Iron

Spray glue and glitter (optional)

Note: Patterns shown are for five different snowflake designs. Each pattern shows ¼ of snowflake.

1. To make typing-paper snowflakes, fold a 4½" square of paper in half, twice.

Trace around snowflake pattern, placing dotted lines on paper folds. Cut out, unfold paper, and iron. If desired, spray with glue and sprinkle with glitter, one side at a time.
2. To make watercolor-paper snowflakes, use tracing paper and trace each ¼ pattern four times, rotating pattern piece to complete the snowflake. Trace onto watercolor paper and cut out.
3. Thread needle with silver thread, insert through one point of snowflake, and loop around top center of each arch. Tie thread ends together or tack to fabric covering arch.

Place Mats and Napkins
Materials:

2½ yds. 44/45"-wide black-and-white checked or plaid fabric (**Note:** Yardage will make six place mats and six napkins.)

Thread to match

Scissors

Sewing machine

1. Cut each place mat 12" x 18". Cut each napkin 18" square.
2. Sew around perimeter of napkins and place mats approximately ½" in from edge. Fringe to stitching.

Reindeer Napkin Holders/Ornaments
Materials:

22" x 30" sheet 140 lb. watercolor paper (**Note:** Sheet will make six reindeer napkin holders.)

3 yds. ¼"-wide red ribbon (18" per deer)

Tracing paper and pencil

Tacky white glue

Silver thread

Hand-sewing needle

Scissors

To make as napkin holders:

1. Trace around deer pattern on watercolor paper. Trace a second deer without antlers for use as a reinforcement.
2. Cut out all deer shapes. Glue reinforcement shapes to backs of complete deer shapes. Let dry. Draw on features if desired. Tie red bow around deer's neck.

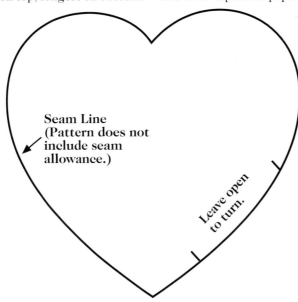

Seam Line (Pattern does not include seam allowance.)

Leave open to turn.

RAGTAG CALICO TREE HEART PATTERN

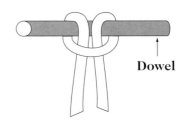

Dowel

LARK'S-HEAD KNOT

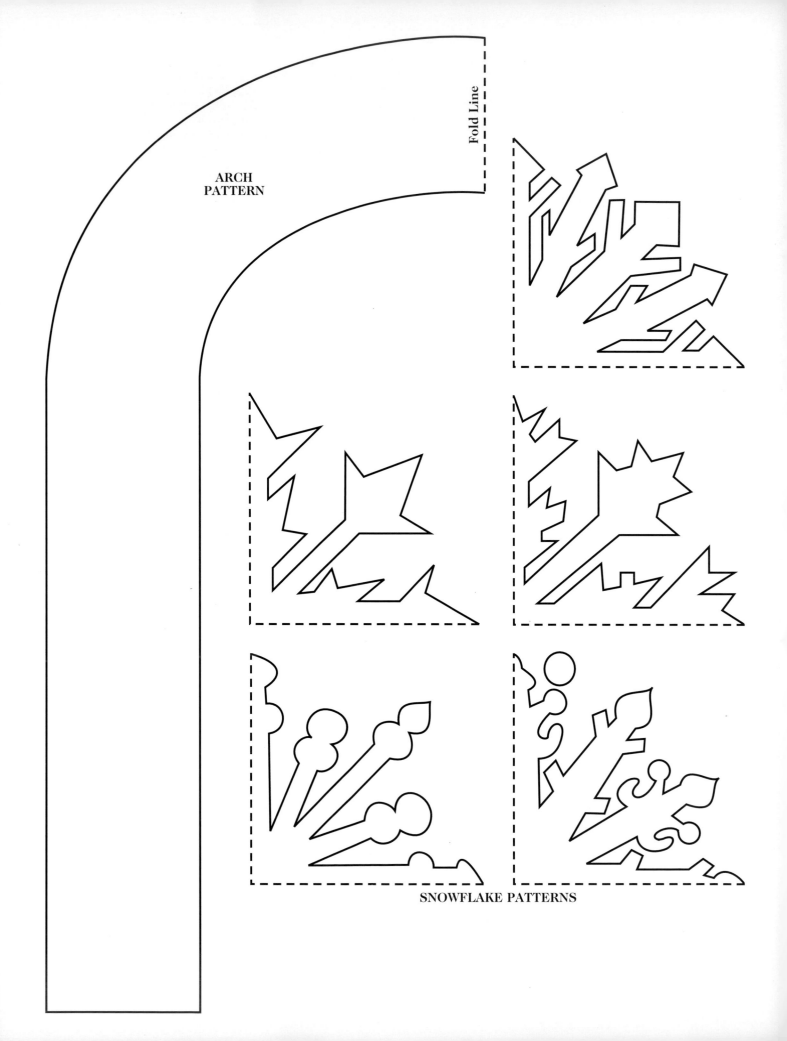

ARCH PATTERN

Fold Line

SNOWFLAKE PATTERNS

To make as ornaments:
1. Trace around deer pattern on water-color paper. Cut out deer shapes.
2. Thread needle with silver thread, insert at *X* on antlers, and tie thread ends together to form hanger.
Note: Felt holly leaves and jingle bells may be added around deer's neck, if desired.

Arches and Snowflakes Centerpiece
Materials:
21" x 27" piece mat board
⅔ yd. 44/45"-wide black moiré fabric
Thread to match
Hand-sewing needle
Heavy utility scissors **or** utility knife (to cut mat board)
Glue
Sewing machine

Option: To achieve a more traditional look with these contemporary pieces, cover the arches with solid or plaid Christmas taffeta. For table decorations at a bridal shower or wedding, cover the arches in white, and hang hearts or flowers from them.

1. Trace five arches onto mat board. Cut out.
2. Cut moiré into five 4½" x 44/45" strips. Fold in half lengthwise, with right sides of fabric together. Sew the long side, forming a tube, using a ⅜" seam allowance. Turn right-side out. Slide tube onto arch, gathering fabric and being careful not to bend arch. Turn raw edges under and glue to arch to secure.
3. Tack arches together at sides near top and bottom, forming hinges.
4. Display arches in a zigzag fashion, so that they will stand upright by themselves.

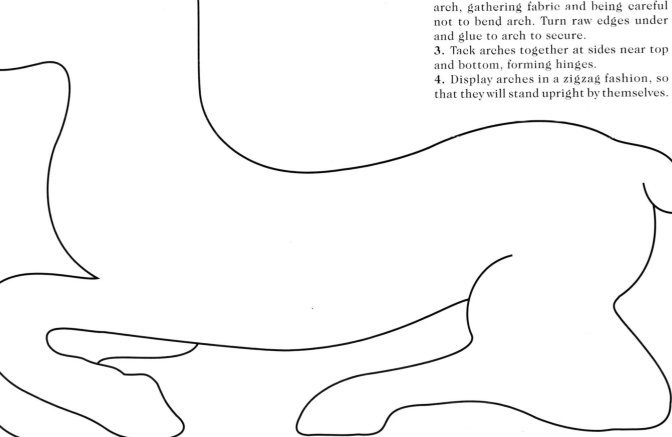

DEER PATTERN

ALL AROUND
THE HOUSE

When it comes to decorating our homes for the holidays, the possibilities are almost endless. From floors to walls to tabletops to banisters, yes banisters, and nearly everything in between, there is something on the following pages for everyone. These projects will help you deck the walls and trim the halls from one end of the house to the other. Whether your favorite pastime is creative crafting, gorgeous quilting, elegant crochet, or classic cross stitch, you're certain to find an assortment of projects that you just can't wait to begin! You'll find folk-art-inspired Papier-Mâché Santas, a traditional, red and green Gifts of Christmas collection, an elegant, white-crochet Celebration Angel, and an eye-catching, Embossed Copper Nativity. There is something here for every taste and decorating spot imaginable.

ALL AROUND THE HOUSE

Decking the Halls

Because Christmastime is our favorite time of the year, we spend hour after hour during the months leading up to the holidays planning and preparing the decorations we will use to adorn our homes throughout the yuletide season. Whether crafted, crocheted, or cross stitched, each project has a special place in our homes and in our hearts. The day we begin "decking the halls" is an occasion that brings family members of all ages together for sharing, caring, laughter, and fun. The house buzzes with the excitement of the season as the aromas of hot cocoa, apple cider, and ginger cookies fill the air.

Above and right—Piles and piles of patchwork pieced from Christmas prints will make your holiday season a pleasurable one. Making these coordinating **Gifts of Christmas** pieces— pillows, tree skirt, and ornaments—will certainly fill you with the Christmas spirit while you fill your house with the warmth and down-home feeling of patchwork. Why not start a gift series for a special friend or family member? Make some ornaments one year, a pair of pillows the next, and keep going until you have filled that lucky person's home with the traditional coziness of patchwork. Your handmade gifts will be eagerly anticipated each year and will light up seasonal festivities for many Christmases to come. Instructions begin on page 75.

Above—This panoramic cross-stitch Nativity scene, titled **Cross-Stitch Crèche,** *beautifully portrays the birth of Jesus in three, freestanding parts. In the center section, Mary kneels over the Christ Child while the watchful Joseph and a curious sheep stand by protectively. The left panel shows two shepherds looking at the scene in innocent wonder. They are accompanied by a lamb, a sheep, and a donkey. The right panel contains the three*

Wise Men, weary from their long journey but in reverent awe of Jesus' birth. The camels have knelt, allowing the Wise Men to present their opulent gifts to the newborn King. All three panels are cleverly finished with a fabric back, polyester filling, and an aquarium-rock-filled fabric base. The resulting pieces will stand on any flat surface. This unusual crèche is certain to become a treasured holiday centerpiece! Charts begin on page 80.

*Above—Simple outlines form the tender scene of the Nativity, with Joseph and Mary cradling Jesus beneath the star. To create this **Embossed Copper Nativity**, you will use items found in most households—embossing tools such as a ballpoint pen, a screwdriver, and a nail. The striking serenity of this Nativity is due, in part, to the simplicity of its lines and the warm glow of the copper. Hang this Nativity on an evergreen branch or from a wooden dowel and add it to your Christmas collection. Instructions begin on page 85.*

62

Above—*The natural look of raffia and twisted paper gives this* **Holy Family** *nativity set a rustic, earthy appearance that will be right at home with country decor. Flowing headdresses for Mary and Joseph are formed by wire-edged ribbon, which will stay the way you shape it and can easily be reshaped as desired. Silk poinsettia leaves add a further touch of nature to the Holy Family as Joseph's collar, Mary's halo, and Baby Jesus' swaddling clothes. Instructions begin on page 87.*

Above and right—This quaint adaptation of the Nativity scene, cut from wood, also includes its own drawstring storage bag, which bears the motto, "Christ Is Born." The simple lines of the pieces that comprise this **Wooden Nativity** will make each piece a pleasure to cut and a joy to paint, from the bright yellow star to the tiny, fleecy sheep. Children will love to play with this cheerful, colorful Nativity set as they learn the story that goes with it. Its storage bag makes the set a great choice to take along on the holiday trip to Grandma's house. Instructions begin on page 89.

Above—These **Papier-Mâché Santas** *are even prettier than the expensive ones found in department stores and specialty shops, and are far more special because they are handmade. One holds a candy cane, one has a sprig of evergreen on his hat, and the third is about to pop down the chimney on Christmas eve. They will look perfect as part of a Christmas centerpiece surrounded by greenery. Instructions begin on page 90.*

Left and below—Garlands of greenery are given extra richness by vivid swags and bows of wire-edged ribbon in three different holiday shades. Red, metallic gold, and Christmas-print ribbons blend as they are twisted and tied the length of the garland to form the eye-catching **Banister Trimmings.** *Faux fruit, including large clusters of grapes, sprays of berries, and sprays of mixed fruit, also contribute to the look of this elegant seasonal decor. Wrap it around your banister for display throughout the holidays, and enjoy the contrast of the greenery and ribbons against the wood of the stairway. Instructions are on page 79.*

Left—For those celebrating Christmas in the South or those who want to add a touch of Southern flavor to their festivities, we present the **Magnolias and Bows** centerpiece, which features magnolias, the creamy-white blossoms that are the state flower of Mississippi. The multiple-loop bow is made from more than four yards of wire-edged, magnolia-patterned ribbon. Just imagine this lovely adornment attached to your banister or used as the center of a greenery swag. The centerpiece is created from silk magnolias, ivy, berries, and greenery placed within a long basket—choose one to complement your decor. If you enjoy working with freshly cut flowers in the spring and summer, you'll love creating this elegant silk arrangement this winter. Instructions begin on page 78.

Above—Simple-to-stitch plastic canvas combined with a traditional quilting design, the Log-Cabin block, results in a colorful Christmas wreath. The geometric look of the **Log-Cabin Wreath** makes it an appropriate decoration for rooms with a contemporary flair, while the classic quilting design contributes a timeless air that will work with any decorating scheme. An interesting feature of this project is the wreath's bow, which is stitched and assembled separately and then added to the wreath after it has been framed. We think this seasonal design will draw the eyes of passersby, who will be certain to comment on your handiwork. Instructions begin on page 100.

Above—Bright, cheery colors will make this cross-stitch piece, titled **Happy Holidays Bells,** the standout of the season. A "Happy Holidays" banner floats above two red-and-yellow bells, with a garland of yellow stars and greenery completing the design. And what a wonderful idea for finishing; display your completed cross stitch in the center opening of an evergreen wreath topped with a large, red bow, and holly and berries. Easy to complete in a small amount of time, this piece will be a fabulous addition to your holiday decorating, and can also make a great gift. We recommend that you hang this beauty indoors, though—remember, the weather outside is frightful! Chart is on page 93.

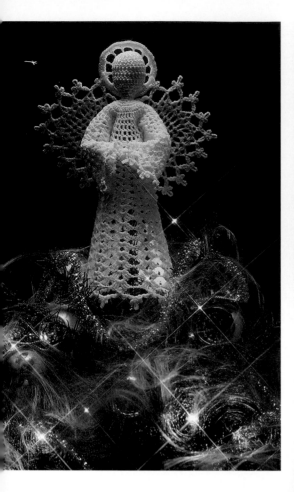

Above and right—Most of us, when we think of crochet, draw a mental picture of lacy doilies and dresser scarves gracing the furniture at Grandma's house. But this elegant needlework need not be limited to those items. Using the same types of materials Grandma used, you can make a **Celebration Angel** for your family to enjoy this year and in years to come. Whether used as a tree topper, shown above, or placed on a tabletop, at right, this crocheted celestial greeter will add a distinctive holiday warmth to her surroundings. Place her in a special spot in your home, or present her to a dear friend. Instructions begin on page 91.

*Above—This quick-to-crochet, beautiful, hearth-side rug is ideal for use at a fireplace or in an entryway. Plan to make several during the summer months and present them to friends for use during the holidays. The large stitch gauge and thick yarn make this **Floral Zigzag Rug** an easy project to make. Instructions are on page 100.*

Above—*A four-block wall hanging is just the right size for a quick Christmas gift or to whip up for your own holiday home. Eight-point stars in roses, greens, blues, and yellows make the* **Starry Christmas Quilt** *festive; and straight seams and simple construction make it a breeze to complete. Choose different fabric colors to match your home's decor, or stick with bright Christmas shades for a traditional holiday wall hanging. Instructions begin on page 95.*

Above—*Two quilt designs, the Schoolhouse and Log-Cabin blocks, are combined to create the delightful* **I'll Be Home for Christmas Quilt.** *Constructed using an assortment of holiday-inspired fabrics, this wall-size charmer is certain to delight all who return home for the holidays this year. If you like the design and would prefer to display this piece throughout the year, substitute fabrics and colors that will complement the decor of your home. Instructions begin on page 96.*

The things you'll need to build a
snowman

tree branches a pipe

lots & lots of snow

coal for the eyes and smile

one carrot

one odd mitten and glove

an old hat

grandma's old scarf

Above—*Just in case you don't remember them, the ingredients for a perfect snowman are listed in this delightful cross-stitch design, titled* **Recipe for a Snowman.** *The finished snowman, complete with rakish top hat, stands in the center; and all around him, his other necessary accessories are shown. Put all those parts together and you'll have a snowman even better than Frosty. Unlike the outdoor variety, you can keep this snowman inside; and he'll never melt! Chart begins on page 94.*

Gifts of Christmas

Gift-Box Pillows
Materials:
½ yd. 44/45"-wide red-and-green plaid fabric (F)
¼ yd. 44/45"-wide ivory print fabric (C, D, and E)
¼ yd. 44/45"-wide red plaid **or** dark green pindot fabric (B and H)
Small scraps light green print fabric, cut into four 2½" squares (G)
Two 2⅝" x 5½" scraps red solid fabric **or** dark green solid fabric (A)
15" square muslin
20" length gold cord
Large gold bead
Clear nylon monofilament
14"-square pillow form **or** 1 medium-size bag polyester filling
15" square batting
Straight pins
Hand-sewing needle
Measuring tape
Scissors
Sewing machine
Iron

Finished size: 14" x 14"
Note: Materials listed will make one *Gift-Box Pillow.* Use a ¼" seam allowance throughout.

1. Cut the following pieces from each fabric:
   A—Two 2⅝" x 5½" pieces
   B—One 1¼" x 5½" piece
   C—Two 3" x 5½" pieces
   D—One 3½" x 10½" piece
   E—One 2½" x 10½" piece
   F—Four 2½" x 10½" pieces
   G—Four 2½"-square pieces
   H—One 2¼" x 26" piece

2. Sew one piece A and piece B together along long sides. Sew second piece A to opposite side of piece B. Sew two C pieces to opposite sides of A/B/A block along long sides, referring to Piecing and Quilting Schematic. Assembled strip should measure 5½" x 10½". Sew strip D to one long side of assembled strip and strip E to opposite side of assembled strip, referring to Piecing and Quilting Schematic. Sew one F strip to each side of assembled block. Sew four G pieces to remaining two F strips along short ends. Sew assembled F/G strips to top and bottom of pieced block.

3. Fold piece H in half along lengthwise edge, placing right sides of fabric together. Sew together along lengthwise edge. Turn right-side out and press. Tuck in raw edges at ends and

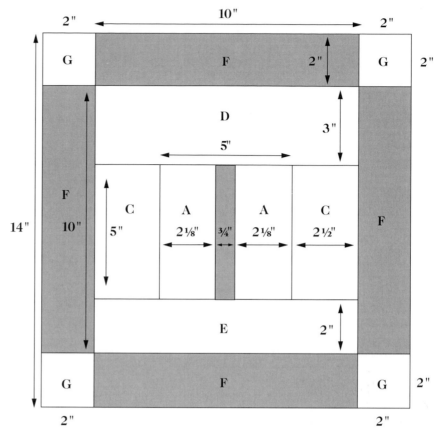

PIECING AND QUILTING SCHEMATIC

slip stitch ends closed. Fold ribbon to form three loops at center, referring to photo on page **58** and leaving ribbon ends as bow streamers. At each fold, use a running stitch to sew the two layers together. Then gather and wrap thread around gathered area tightly and knot securely. From back of pillow top, sew center of ribbon to center top of section B. Arrange loops and streamers as desired and tack ends and loops in place from back.

4. Tie small loop knot in each end of gold cord. Fold cord to form a bow and tack to center of fabric ribbon, using clear nylon monofilament. Sew gold bead to center of gold-cord bow.

5. Place muslin backing, batting, and pillow top (right-side up) atop a flat surface. Baste layers together. Quilt along outside of gift box ⅛" away from seam lines and along borders ⅛" away from seam lines. Trim edges even with pillow top.

6. Cut square from red-and-green plaid to match size of assembled pillow top. Pin backing to pillow top, placing right sides of fabric together and aligning raw edges. Sew together, leaving an 8" opening for turning and stuffing. Clip corners, turn right-side out, and stuff with pillow form or polyester filling. Whipstitch opening closed.

Ornament Collection
Note: For these projects, a general materials list has been given. Specific materials for each project have been listed separately. Use a ¼" seam allowance throughout. Use 100% cotton fabric.

General materials:
Colored pencil **or** chalk
Tracing paper and pencil
Polyester filling
Straight pins
Hand-sewing needle
Scissors
Iron
Sewing machine (optional)

Stockings and Hearts
Materials:
Fourteen–sixteen 12" or longer strips assorted, complementary, Christmas-print fabrics in assorted widths of your choice
Three 4" x 6" scraps Christmas-print fabric (for backing for stockings)
Three 4"-square scraps Christmas-print fabric (for backing for hearts)
Thread to match fabrics
1¾ yds. ⅜"-wide red satin ribbon, cut into 10½" lengths (for hangers)

Note: Materials listed will make three *Stocking* ornaments and three *Heart* ornaments.

1. Cut out patterns for stocking and heart.

2. Arrange 12"-long fabric strips in a random, pleasing order atop a flat surface. Sew strips together along lengthwise edges to form a 12" square. Turn to wrong side and press seams open or toward darker fabrics. Place paper patterns atop right side of pieced fabric square and draw around templates, using colored pencil or chalk.

3. Place patterns atop right side of backing-fabric squares and cut one backing piece for each ornament. (**Note:** For stockings, flip pattern to wrong side before cutting fabric.) Pin backing and pieced front with right sides of fabric together, aligning raw edges. Sew shapes together, leaving an opening for turning. (**Note:** For *Stocking*, leave top open. For *Heart*, leave one straight side open.) Remove pins. Clip curves and turn right-side out. Press, shape, and stuff with polyester filling.

4. Fold each 10½" length of ribbon in half and tie a knot ½" from cut ends. For stockings, insert ribbon loop into top opening at heel side of stocking and whipstitch opening closed. For hearts, sew ribbon knot to back of ornament at top center of heart. Whipstitch opening closed.

Packages
Materials:
⅛ yd. 44/45"-wide Christmas-print fabric
Thread to match
3¼ yds. ⅜"-wide red satin ribbon
⅛ yd. fusible web
4 Mill Hill glass pebble beads, color: gold #05557

Note: Materials listed will make four *Package* ornaments.

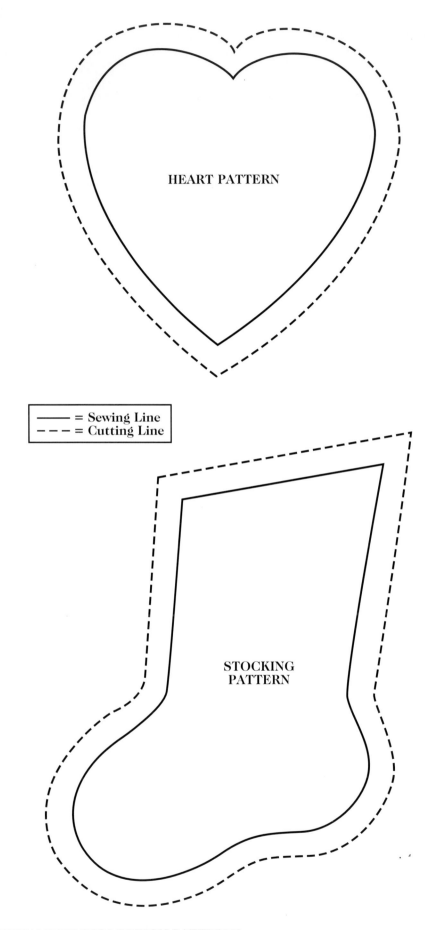

HEART PATTERN

= Sewing Line
- - - = Cutting Line

STOCKING PATTERN

HEART APPLIQUE PATTERN

ORNAMENT COLLECTION PATTERNS

1. Cut four 7" x 3½" pieces from Christmas-print fabric.

2. Cut fusible web into four 7" x ¼" strips. Fuse web to ribbon, following manufacturer's instructions for fusing. Fuse ribbon lengthwise down center of fabric pieces.

3. Fold fabric in half with right sides together, forming a square. Pin and sew together down each side. Turn right-side out and press. Turn top, raw edge under ¼" and press. Stuff ornament with polyester filling. Whipstitch top closed.

4. Cut ribbon into four 28" lengths. Fold one length in half. Make a tight, looped knot 2½" from fold to form hanger. Tie bow from streamers and sew bow securely to top of package. Sew one gold bead to bow's knot.

Heart Appliqué
Materials:
⅛ yd. 44/45"-wide dark green pindot fabric
⅛ yd. 44/45"-wide red solid fabric
2 yds. ⅜"-wide red satin ribbon
Tweezers
Small piece freezer paper

Note: Materials listed will make three *Heart Appliqué* ornaments.

1. Cut two 3½" squares from dark green pindot fabric. Trace heart pattern onto paper side of freezer paper and cut out. Press freezer paper shiny-side down to wrong side of red fabric, using iron. Cut heart from red fabric, adding a ¼" seam allowance to fabric when cutting.

2. Press seam allowance to freezer-paper side of fabric. Appliqué one red heart to center of one dark green pindot square, turning raw edges of heart under. Before completing appliqué, use tweezers to remove freezer paper from behind heart. Finish appliquéing heart to square.

3. Sew one appliquéd fabric square to one plain fabric square, placing right sides of fabric together, aligning raw edges, and leaving 1½" open at top for turning. Clip corners and turn right-side out. Press. Stuff with polyester filling. Whipstitch opening closed.

4. Cut 10½" length from ribbon. Knot ribbon ¾" from each end. Tack knots to front of ornament at upper corners. Cut another 10½" length from ribbon, tie in a bow, and sew to upper-left corner of ornament at knot.

5. Repeat Steps 1–4 for remaining ornaments.

Pinwheels
Materials:
⅛ yd. 44/45"-wide red fabric
⅛ yd. 44/45"-wide blue plaid fabric
Thread to match fabrics
1 yd. ⅜"-wide red satin ribbon
3 Mill Hill glass pebble beads, color: gold #05557

Note: Materials listed will make three *Pinwheel* ornaments.

1. Cut six 2⅜" squares from each fabric. Cut three 3½" squares from red fabric only. Cut 2⅜" squares in half diagonally to form 12 triangles of each fabric. Sew one red and one blue triangle together along long side to form square. Press seam open. Repeat for remaining triangles. Sew two pieced squares together at opposite colors to form strip. Make six strips. Sew two strips together at opposite colors to form pinwheel square. Make three pinwheel squares.

2. Sew one gold bead to center of each pinwheel square.

3. Pin 3½" red square atop one pinwheel square, placing right sides of fabric together and aligning raw edges. Sew around square, leaving a 1½" opening for turning. Remove pins. Clip corners, turn right-side out, and press. (**Note:** When pressing, be careful not to touch bead with hot iron.) Stuff with polyester filling. Whipstitch opening closed.

4. Cut a 10½" length from ribbon. Fold in half and tie a loop knot ½" from end. Tack knot to back of ornament at one corner.

Pinwheel and Yo-Yo Tree Skirt
Materials:
1⅛ yds. 44/45"-wide muslin fabric (for backing)
1¼ yds. 44/45"-wide navy plaid fabric
¾ yd. 44/45"-wide red solid fabric
¾ yd. 44/45"-wide dark green pindot fabric
¼ yd. 44/45"-wide ivory print fabric
1 pkg. 45" x 60" thin quilt batting
4 yds. ¾"-wide lace edging
16 Mill Hill glass pebble beads, color: gold #05557
Eight ½" jingle bells, color: gold
2 large metal snaps
26" length string
Transparent **or** masking tape
17" x 34" sheet of paper (**Note:** Tape four 11" x 17" pieces of paper together to make one large sheet.)
Hand-sewing needle
Yardstick
Pencil
Straight pins
Scissors
Thread
Iron
1 yd. Pellon® Wonder-Under® Transfer Web (optional)
Sewing machine (optional)

Note: Materials listed will make one *Pinwheel and Yo-Yo Tree Skirt*. Use a ¼" seam allowance throughout. Use 100% cotton fabrics.

1. Cut along edges of backing fabric to form a 36" square. Fold fabric in half and then in quarters. Knot string tightly around pencil, near writing end, and tape in place. Tie a tight loop 18" away from pencil and pin knot at folded center of fabric. Mark a quarter circle along edge of folded fabric, using pencil and string as a compass.
Note: Be sure to keep pencil perpendicular to fabric or line will not be accurate.

2. Pin fabric near marked circle to hold in place and cut away excess fabric along curve. Remove pin from knot and tie a knot 2½" from pencil. Use to make a small, inner circle at corner of fabric and cut away excess fabric from center.

3. Unfold fabric from quarters to halves. Mark dots along one folded edge of fabric, ¾" away from fold at top circle and 2½" away from fold at bottom. Draw a line between dots and cut along line through both thicknesses. This step removes a small segment of fabric to form skirt opening. Place cut edges together and fold and press remaining fabric into halves, then quarters, then eighths.

4. While fabric is folded, place atop paper and trace carefully around shape. Add ½" around perimeter of outline. (**Note:** This will form pattern for tree-skirt panels.) Unfold fabric. On wrong side of fabric, use a yardstick and pencil to draw heavy lines along each fold to mark stitching lines. Cut out paper pattern and use to cut four navy, two red, and two green panels for tree skirt. On wrong side of each panel, mark a stitching line ½" in from edge along long edges. Set aside backing fabric and fabric panels.

5. Make pinwheel patches by cutting strips of fabric 3⅞" wide and cutting strips into squares as follows:
    Cut 16 squares from ivory print fabric;

Cut 8 squares from solid red fabric;
Cut 4 squares from green pindot fabric;
Cut 4 squares from navy plaid fabric. Cut each square in half diagonally to form two triangles.

6. Make pinwheel patch edging strips by cutting strips of fabric as follows:
Cut four 1½" x 7" strips and four 1½" x 9" strips from red solid fabric;
Cut four 1½" x 7" strips and four 1½" x 9" strips from navy plaid fabric;
Cut eight 1½" x 7" strips and eight 1½" x 9" strips from green pin-dot fabric.

Note: Each pinwheel patch requires two edging strips 7" long and two edging strips 9" long.

7. For each patch, place four ivory triangles and four triangles of another color fabric with right sides of fabric together, referring to photo on page **59** for fabric placement. Sew triangles together along long edges to form squares. Press seams open and trim away excess fabric at corners. Lay the four pieced squares atop a flat surface to form a pinwheel shape, referring to photo for placement. Sew together the two squares on the top and then the two squares on the bottom. Press seams open. Sew top section to bottom section, being careful to match seams at center. Press seam open.

8. To add edging, pin two 7"-long strips on opposite sides of patch, placing right sides of fabric together and aligning raw edges. Sew together, remove pins, and press seam open. Trim away excess fabric at ends. Pin two 9"-long strips on remaining sides of patch, placing right sides of fabric together and aligning raw edges. Sew together, remove pins, and press seam open. Fold and press edging strips under neatly so that ⅝" remains showing around edges of patch. Repeat for each pinwheel patch.

9. Center one pinwheel patch on each skirt section, placing point ¾" from bottom edge and referring to photo for color placement. Machine or hand appliqué patches to panels.

Option: Patches may be fused to panels using Wonder-Under®. If using this method, follow manufacturer's instructions for fusing.

10. Place fabric backing piece atop a large, flat surface and completely cover with quilt batting. Smooth and pin backing and batting together, being careful not to stretch batting. Baste backing and batting together ¼" in from all edges, using long running stitches. Trim away excess batting.

11. Turn skirt so that batting layer is on the bottom and opening is toward you. Place one navy plaid skirt section right-side down at left-hand side of opening. Match raw edges and pin in place. Sew along vertical seam line through all three layers. Turn navy plaid section so that right side of fabric is up and it covers batting. Place a red section right-side down atop navy plaid section, aligning raw edges and placing marked seam lines along heavy pencil line, which will be visible through batting. Pin in place and sew through all four layers along seam line. Flip red section right-side up. Repeat process to add each section of skirt, adding a navy plaid section to red section, then adding a green pindot section, another navy plaid section, another red section, another navy plaid section, and another green pindot section.

12. At last section edge along skirt opening, turn raw edge of fabric under, fold around batting to backing, and whipstitch in place. At center opening of skirt, fold raw edge under and whipstitch to backing. Around outer edge of skirt, baste all layers together along previous basting stitches. Turn raw edges under, fold to back of skirt, and whipstitch in place. Sew lace along outer edge of tree skirt, allowing lace to extend beyond edge of skirt. Steam press lace for center opening into a circular shape and then sew in place.

13. Cut eight fabric circles approximately 3½" in diameter from ivory print fabric. Use a running stitch to sew around each circle, folding edge under ⅛"–¼" as you go. Pull up threads tightly, pulling fabric into a circle, and flatten to make yo-yo. Sew closed and sew a gold bead at center. Sew one yo-yo to skirt at each point where pinwheel patches join. At skirt opening, sew a yo-yo to point of left patch only.

14. Sew a gold bead at upper corner of each patch and a jingle bell at lower corner of each patch, sewing jingle bells over lace edging. Sew snaps to both sides of skirt opening at center top and at juncture of patches underneath yo-yo.

Magnolias and Bows

Magnolia Arrangement
Materials:
Purchased 12" x 8" x 4" wicker basket
8" x 3½" x 4" block STYROFOAM brand plastic foam
6 silk magnolia blooms with stems (**Note:** Designer used silk magnolia

bush and cut off stems for blooms and buds.)
3 silk magnolia buds with stems
Five 14" silk ivy stems
Two 12" silk ivy stems
Red berry picks, two **each**: 21" long, 18" long, 12" long
Four 18"-long evergreen sprays
Spanish moss
24-gauge wire
9 florist picks
Wire cutters
Green florist tape
Silk magnolia leaves (optional)

1. Attach Styrofoam® block securely to inside of basket, using wire. Cover Styrofoam® with Spanish moss.
2. Insert stems of evergreen sprays into top of Styrofoam® block, arranging along back edge in a fan shape measuring 16" high x 25" wide. Add 14" ivy stems to arrangement, placing ivy stems between, but just in front of, evergreen sprays.
3. Wire stems of magnolia blooms to florist picks to make one 20" stem, one 15" stem, two 16" stems, and two 12" stems. Wire stems of magnolia buds to florist picks to make one 12" stem and two 15" stems. Wrap florist tape around stems and florist picks.
4. To add magnolia blooms to arrangement, refer to photo on page **66** and insert 20" stem into Styrofoam®, positioning toward back and in center, just in front of ivy. On each side of 20" stem, add one 16" stem and then one 12" stem to form line across top of Styrofoam® block in front of ivy and evergreen. Insert 15" stem into Styrofoam®, directly in front of 20" stem. To add magnolia buds to arrangement, insert 12" stem into Styrofoam®, directly in front of 15" bloom stem. Add one 15" bud stem to each side of 15" bloom stem.
5. Referring to photo, insert 21" and 18" berry picks into Styrofoam® between magnolia blooms. Add one 12" berry pick to each side of center bud.
6. To complete arrangement, insert one 12" ivy stem on each side of berry pick at front of basket.

Note: Fill in open areas of arrangement with magnolia leaves, if desired.

Floral Bows
Materials:
4⅓ yds. 2½"-wide wire-edged floral-print ribbon (**Note:** Designer used W. F. R. Ribbon, Inc., Magnolia.)
6" length 24-gauge wire
12"-long red chenille stem

Scissors
Measuring tape

1. Cut 1 yard of ribbon and set aside for streamers.
2. Measure 6" from end of ribbon and crimp to mark center of bow. Measure 6" of remaining ribbon, bring to back of center, crimp edges together, and twist ribbon so right side is up. (**Note:** Each time you bring a loop to the center, twist ribbon so that the right side will be up for the next loop.) Repeat to make loop on opposite side of center of bow. Continue making loops on left and right of bow's center until all ribbon is shaped into loops. Secure center of bow with wire, twisting tightly.
3. To add streamers to bow, crimp center of 1 yd. length of ribbon and attach to center of back of bow, using chenille stem.
4. Shape loops of bow and trim ends of streamers.

Banister Trimmings

Banister Decorations
Materials:
Large silk grape-leaf bush (**Note:** Grape-leaf bush used for model had six runners 20"–24" long and 18 runners 10"–12" long.)
22"-long silk spray with large red berries
12"-long fruit spray
Two 20"-long gold silk spruce sprays
3 large clusters light green grapes
2½ yds. Christmas-print wire-edged ribbon (**Note:** Designer used W. F. R. Ribbon, Inc., Christmas Potpourri.)
2½ yds. red wire-edged ribbon (**Note:** Designer used W. F. R. Ribbon, Inc., Red Moiré.)
2½ yds. gold wire-edged ribbon (**Note:** Designer used W. F. R. Ribbon, Inc., Gold.)
Four 12"-long green chenille stems
24-gauge wire
Wire cutters
Scissors
Yardstick

Note: Materials listed will make one *Banister Decoration.* Finished project is 36" long and 18" across top and tapers toward bottom.

1. Lay grape-leaf bush atop work surface. Fold three long runners to **each** side of stem, leaving remaining runners upright. Wire a gold spruce spray on either side of stem, with limbs pointing down.

Note: If unable to find gold spruce, spray available spruce gold.
2. Wire berry spray onto lower end of stem, placing so that end of spray extends approximately 6" beyond bottom of spruce.
3. Wire fruit spray atop other two (spruce and berry) sprays.
Note: End of fruit spray will be approximately 4" shorter than berry spray.
4. Wire one cluster of grapes at top of **each** spruce spray. Wire remaining cluster of grapes in center of fruit spray, toward bottom of spray.
5. Wrap a chenille stem around top of grape-leaf-bush stem where runners begin, twisting ends together to form a hanging loop.
Note: Later, when ready to attach decoration to banister, twist two–three chenille stems together, insert through loop, and wrap around post.
6. Fold three long runners down on each side and weave into decoration. Wire in place if necessary.
7. To make bow, layer the three ribbon pieces together with right sides up. Hold one end (three ribbons together) and fold over 14". Wrap remainder of ribbon around this folded piece, keeping edges of ribbons straight. Crimp center and wire securely. (**Note:** There should be 7" loops on either side of center.) Wrap a chenille stem over wire. Beginning with inside loops on one side of center, pull one loop to the right and one to the left, until all loops are pulled out. Repeat for remaining side. Attach bow to stem between grapes and hanger. Adjust loops of bow as desired.
Note: Because this ribbon has wire edges, the loops can be adjusted to almost any position.
8. Fold some of the shorter runners down to achieve desired effect. If decoration looks too full at top, trim or remove some of the runners.

Garland
Materials:
9' silk spruce garland
12–14 sprigs silk grape leaves
4½–5 yds. Christmas-print wire-edged ribbon (**Note:** Designer used W. F. R. Ribbon, Inc., Christmas Potpourri.)
4½–5 yds. red wire-edged ribbon (**Note:** Designer used W. F. R. Ribbon, Inc., Red Moiré.)
4½–5 yds. gold wire-edged ribbon (**Note:** Designer used W. F. R. Ribbon, Inc., Gold.)
Green chenille stems
24-gauge wire
Wire cutters
Scissors

Note: Materials listed will make one *Garland.*

1. Place grape leaves along spruce garland and wire in place.
2. Layer the three ribbon pieces together with right sides up. Wrap around garland, securing ends with wire. Trim ends of ribbons.
3. Attach garland to staircase with chenille stems; "fluff" garland.

Cross-Stitch Crèche

	DMC	Color
●	936	avocado, vy. dk.
ഗ	469	avocado
∢	471	avocado, vy. lt.
C	472	avocado, ul. lt.
6	3350	dusty rose, vy. dk.
O	3774	flesh, vy. lt.
∪	754	peach flesh, lt.
■	3371	black-brown
✳	814	garnet, dk.
▲	498	red, dk.
●	792	cornflower, dk.
∠	791	cornflower, vy. dk.
⌐	793	cornflower, med.
◐	699	green
↗	321	red
✕	434	brown, lt.
ı	3072	beaver gray, vy. lt.
·	white	white
X	648	beaver gray, lt.
⊖	647	beaver gray, med.
⍺	783	gold
H	743	yellow, med.
∴	745	yellow, lt. pl.
⌐	3761	sky blue, lt.
+	519	sky blue
∅	518	Wedgwood, lt.
★	801	coffee, dk.
M	995	electric blue, dk.
⍀	809	delft
▽	799	delft, med.
N	300	mahogany, vy. dk.
e	552	violet, dk.
3	208	lavender, vy. dk.
–	739	tan, ul. lt.
L	676	old gold, lt.
∧	738	tan, vy. lt.
⊙	436	tan
8⌐	648	beaver gray, lt.
	white	white
bs	310	black
bs	934	avocado-black

Fabric: 16-count shell Aida from Wichelt Imports, Inc.
Stitch count:

Crèche	114H x 140W
Shepherds	112H x 87W
Wise Men	116H x 122W

(Color code continues on page **83**.)

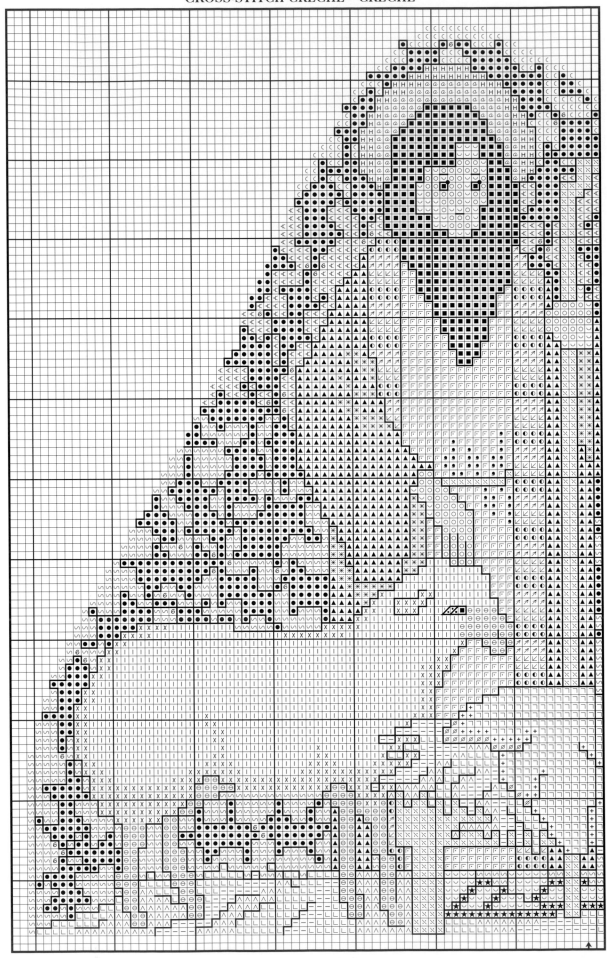

Shaded portion indicates overlap from previous page.

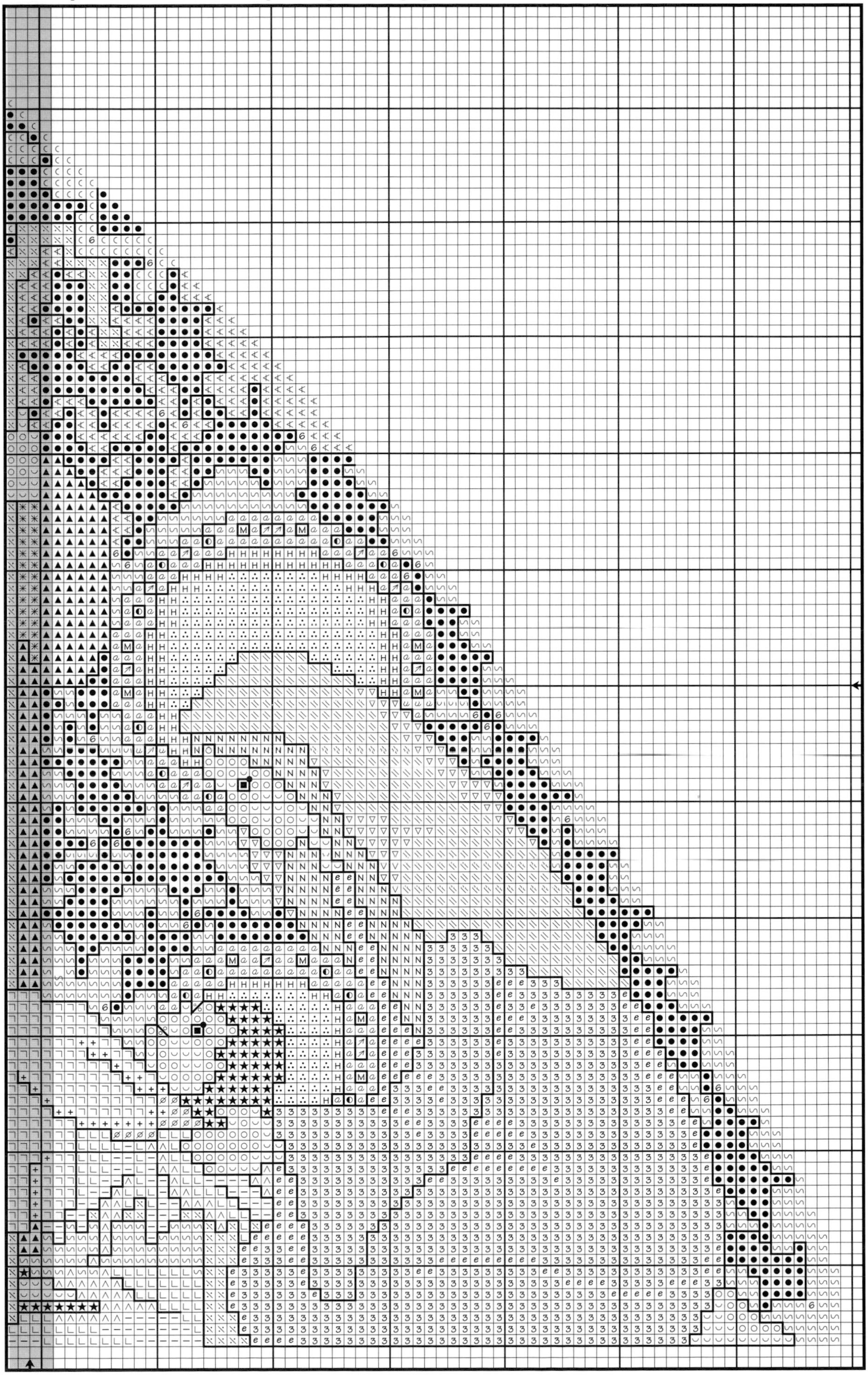

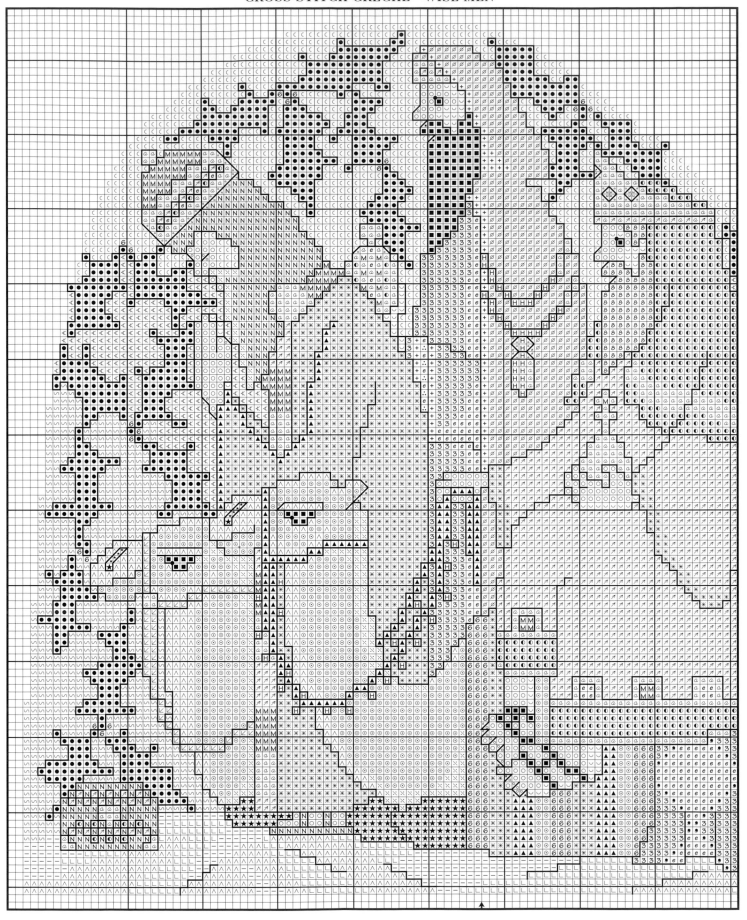

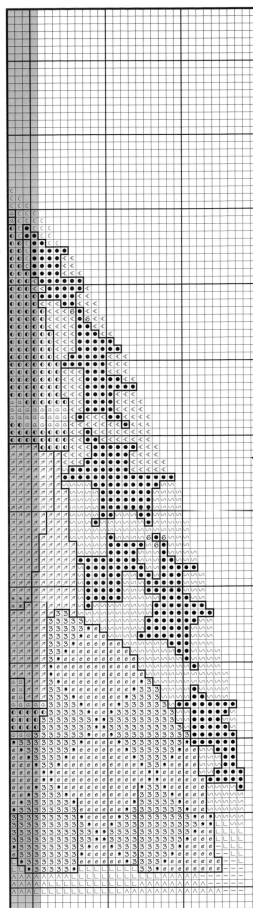

Shaded portion indicates overlap from previous page.

Design size:

Crèche

14-count	8⅛" x 10"
16-count	7⅛" x 8¾"
18-count	6⅜" x 7¾"
22-count	5⅛" x 6⅜"

Shepherds

14-count	8" x 6¼"
16-count	7" x 5⅜"
18-count	6¼" x 4⅞"
22-count	5" x 4"

Wise Men

14-count	8¼" x 8¾"
16-count	7¼" x 7⅝"
18-count	6½" x 6¾"
22-count	5¼" x 5½"

Instructions: Cross stitch using two strands of floss. Backstitch (bs) using one strand of floss. Make French knots where • appears at intersecting grid lines, using one strand white and wrapping floss around needle once.

Backstitch (bs) instructions:

434	hay in manger and on ground
934	holly leaves in background
310	remainder of backstitching

Materials:

¼–½ yd. 44/45"-wide complementary
 fabric (for backing)
Thread to match
⅛ yd. 44/45"-wide muslin **or** other
 tightly woven fabric
Polyester filling
⅛ yd. **or** large scrap stiff fusible in-
 terfacing
One 8-oz. pkg. aquarium rocks **or**
 small pebbles
10" x 12" scrap heavy cardboard
Measuring tape
Scissors
Straight pins
Pencil
Terry-cloth towel
Hand-sewing needle
Sewing machine
Iron

1. Complete stitching following instructions given.
2. Steam press each stitched piece
face-down atop terry-cloth towel. Place each piece face-down atop backing fabric and pin in place. Cut each backing-fabric piece the size of the stitched piece and its surrounding fabric. Machine sew around perimeter of each cross-stitch design along sides and top of figures, placing stitches one row in from edge of cross-stitch design and leaving bottom open. Press along seam line.

3. Trim seam allowances to ½". Notch seam allowance along curves, cutting close to, but not through, stitched line. Turn right-side out, pushing out figures along seam line. Press along edges. Mark bottom seam line across backing fabric.

4. Use base pattern to cut two pieces from muslin. Sew pieces together, using a ¼" seam allowance and leaving an opening for turning. Clip curves and turn right-side out. Fill muslin base with aquarium rocks **or** small pebbles and sew opening closed. Set aside.

5. From base pattern, cut one piece of backing fabric and one piece of fusible interfacing, cutting interfacing minus the ¼" seam allowance. Fuse interfacing to fabric base, following manufacturer's instructions for fusing. Fold seam allowances up over interfacing and press all around. Baste bottom front edge of figures to one edge of fabric base, basting one row in from edge, basting in seam allowance along edge of interfacing, and placing right sides of fabric together. (**Note:** This step will require some turning and manipulation of the fabric. It is important to match centers and helpful to pin pieces together.) Machine sew along basted line and press. Remove basting threads.

6. Stuff figure firmly with polyester filling, leaving space at the bottom and inserting rock-filled base. Cut a piece of heavy cardboard, using base pattern minus seam allowance, and insert just above bottom, fabric base. Trim cardboard as needed to fit into space. Fold bottom, fabric base up to meet back seam line, turning seam allowance under, and whipstitch base and backing together.

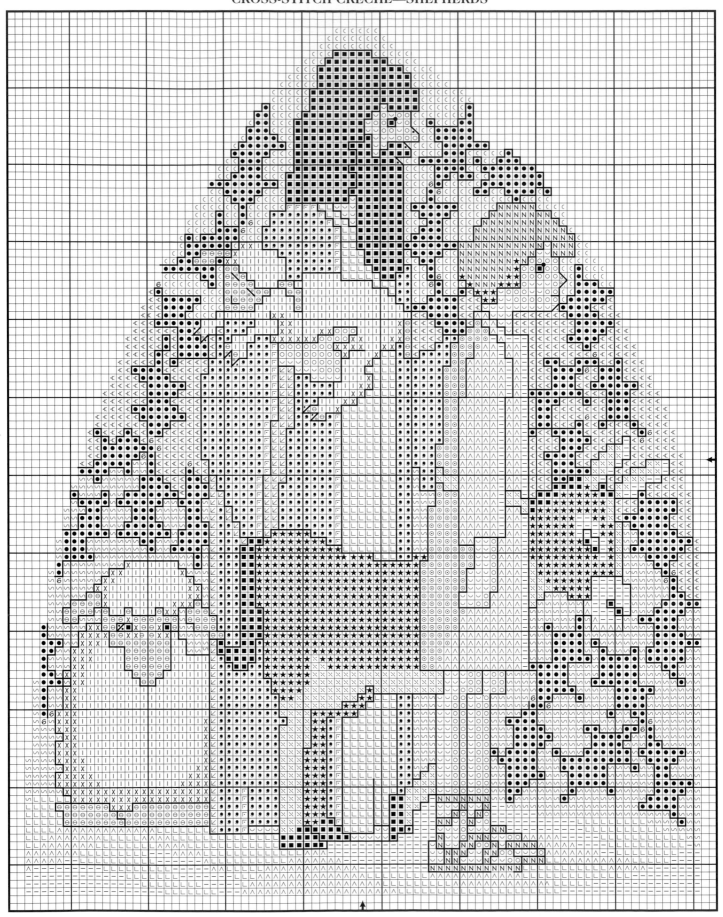

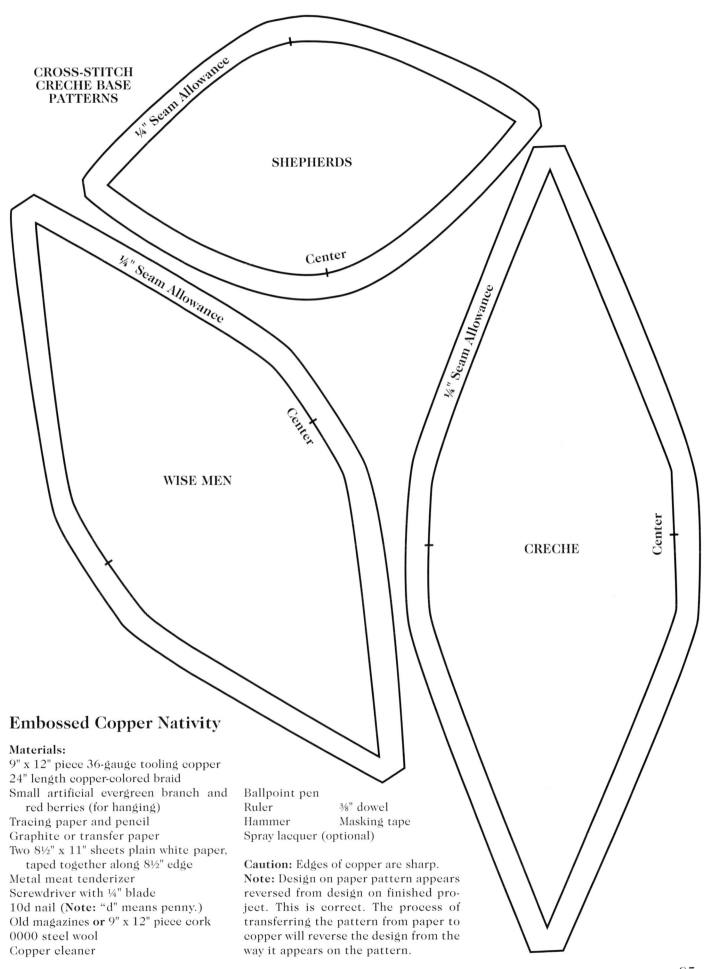

**CROSS-STITCH
CRECHE BASE
PATTERNS**

¼" Seam Allowance

SHEPHERDS

Center

¼" Seam Allowance

Center

¼" Seam Allowance

WISE MEN

CRECHE

Center

Embossed Copper Nativity

Materials:
9" x 12" piece 36-gauge tooling copper
24" length copper-colored braid
Small artificial evergreen branch and
red berries (for hanging)
Tracing paper and pencil
Graphite or transfer paper
Two 8½" x 11" sheets plain white paper,
taped together along 8½" edge
Metal meat tenderizer
Screwdriver with ¼" blade
10d nail (**Note:** "d" means penny.)
Old magazines **or** 9" x 12" piece cork
0000 steel wool
Copper cleaner

Ballpoint pen
Ruler   ⅜" dowel
Hammer   Masking tape
Spray lacquer (optional)

Caution: Edges of copper are sharp.
Note: Design on paper pattern appears reversed from design on finished project. This is correct. The process of transferring the pattern from paper to copper will reverse the design from the way it appears on the pattern.

TOP

H

H

Match dots to continue pattern.

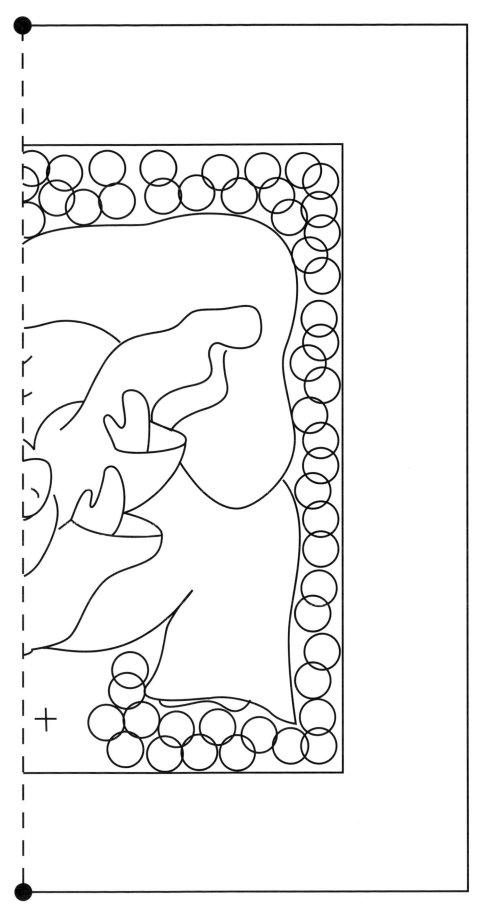

1. Place copper on firmly padded surface such as an old magazine or piece of cork. Emboss straight lines for border 1¼" in from all sides, using ruler and ballpoint pen. Press hard to make a deeply embossed line.

2. Trace pattern onto plain white paper, using tracing paper and pencil. Place graphite paper coated-side down atop copper and tape white paper pattern right-side up atop graphite paper, placing pattern within embossed borders. Lightly trace Holy Family figures and large star. Remove pattern and graphite. Design should be faintly visible.

3. Emboss design, using ballpoint pen and heavy pressure to go over traced lines that form figures. Use ruler for large star.

4. Embellish by using various tools to emboss copper. To form Baby Jesus' halo, gently tap nail with hammer to make dots. (**Note:** Too hard a tap will pierce copper.) For designs in four corners, hold meat tenderizer at each corner and tap with hammer. Tap ⅜" dowel with hammer to make circles in lower part of design, letting circles overlap. To make small stars, tap screwdriver, placing blade horizontally and then vertically, to make +s.

5. Polish copper, if necessary, keeping copper flat while applying any pressure so as not to bend it. Burnish copper by gently rubbing surface, using 0000 steel wool and rubbing in a circular motion.

Option: To preserve shine, spray copper with lacquer and let dry.

Note: Model was not sprayed with lacquer. Sprayed copper is much more difficult to polish than unsprayed, should it tarnish.

6. To hang, tap two holes where indicated by *H*s on pattern, using hammer and nail. Cut two 12" pieces copper-colored braid. Thread one piece of braid through one hole and tie braid ends in a knot to form hanger. Repeat with remaining piece of braid. Loop hangers over branch.

Holy Family

Note: For these projects, a general materials list has been given. Specific materials for each project have been listed separately.

General materials:
Small spool 24-gauge wire
Aleene's Thick Designer Tacky Glue™
Old scissors (for cutting wire)
White glue
Brass sequin pins
Straight pins

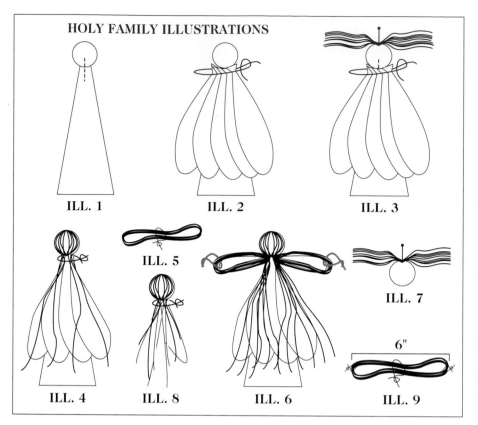

HOLY FAMILY ILLUSTRATIONS

ILL. 1

ILL. 2

ILL. 3

ILL. 5

ILL. 4

ILL. 8

ILL. 6

ILL. 7

6"

ILL. 9

Materials:

Joseph

18" STYROFOAM brand plastic foam cone with 5" base

2½" x 3½" STYROFOAM brand plastic foam egg

2½ yds. burgundy twisted paper

2 oz. natural raffia

Large silk poinsettia bush with burgundy petals approximately 4" long

1 yd. 3"-wide wire-edged burgundy-and-green silk ribbon

Brown grocery bag

Mary

15" STYROFOAM brand plastic foam cone with 4" base

2½" x 3½" STYROFOAM brand plastic foam egg

2 yds. blue twisted paper

2 oz. natural raffia

14" length 16-gauge wire

1 yd. 2"-wide wire-edged metallic-gold ribbon

Brown grocery bag

5 blue forget-me-not silk blossoms

Five 2"-long petals from blue silk flower

5 poinsettia leaves **each** 4" long

Baby Jesus

1½" STYROFOAM brand plastic foam ball

1 oz. natural raffia

Purple silk mum 3" in diameter

3 poinsettia leaves **each** 2" long

Note: *Joseph* is approximately 22" tall. *Mary* is approximately 18" tall.

Option: This project could be made using dried flowers instead of silk for a completely different look. If using dried flowers, figures will be very fragile—be sure to take special precautions when handling and storing them so that they will last more than one season.

1. To prepare cones for *Mary* and *Joseph*, cut brown bags loosely to fit around cones to cover them. Crumple bags and then smooth out. Spread white glue all over both Styrofoam® cones and press on paper. Let dry. Trim off excess paper.

2. To attach heads, put generous dab of Tacky Glue at top of cone. Cut two 7" lengths of wired stem from poinsettia bush. Push half of one stem into bottom of one Styrofoam® egg and other half into top of one cone, attaching egg to top of cone to form head. Refer to Illustration 1. Repeat for remaining cone and egg.

3. For *Joseph*, cut five 18" lengths of burgundy twisted paper and untwist it. Round off one end of each piece. Hold unrounded ends in place around neck of cone and wrap with 6" length of 24-gauge wire to secure, referring to Illustration 2. For *Mary*, cut four 14" lengths blue twisted paper and untwist it. Round off one end of each piece. Secure at neck as for *Joseph*.

4. To cover each head, spread Tacky Glue all over head. For **each** head, hold 30 strands of 40"-long raffia together in center of strands. Twist once. Use a

straight pin to hold twist in top of each head and spread raffia strands around head from center top until head is completely covered, referring to Illustrations 3 and 4. Let dry. Use 6" length of wire to wrap around raffia and pull in at neck. Twist wire to secure, leaving raffia tails loose and hanging over cones.

5. To make arms, fold 20 strands raffia in half and then in half again for **each** figure. Twist 12" length of wire around center of strands, pulling tightly to secure. Refer to Illustration 5. Twist this wire around neck of figure to secure arms to body. Form each wrist by twisting a 4" length of wire around each end loop and pulling tightly, referring to Illustration 6. Twist to secure. Cut off wire and tuck ends up into raffia.

6. To make *Joseph*'s collar, cut three leaves and five large and four small petals from poinsettia. Use Tacky Glue to attach petals in a fan shape around neck. Glue bracts ("berries" from poinsettia) atop small burgundy petals. Tuck and glue three green leaves beneath burgundy petals. Drape wire-edged, burgundy-and-green silk ribbon over head, pinning in place with sequin pins.

7. To make *Mary*'s collar, cut five blue silk petals and glue around neck in a fan shape. Glue five blue forget-me-nots above blue petals. Cut five leaves from poinsettia bush and glue to back of head in a fan shape.

8. To make *Baby Jesus*, cover 1½" Styrofoam® ball with Tacky Glue. Fold five strands raffia in half and then in half again. Twist raffia in center and cover head as for *Joseph* and *Mary*, referring to Illustration 7. Let dry. Use 6" length of wire to pull in and tie under ball to make neck, referring to Illustration 8. Let remaining strands of raffia hang loose. To make arms, fold five strands raffia, referring to Illustration 9. Wire center to secure, and wire to neck. Use one piece of wire to loop through both end loops and tie them together as if hands were clasped. Trim wire and push ends up into raffia. Disassemble purple mum. Clip into two layers of petals and glue two layers around *Baby Jesus*' neck. Glue one smaller circle of petals atop head. Glue three small poinsettia leaves under arms to suggest swaddling clothes.

9. Insert 14" length of 16-gauge wire horizontally through top of cone part of *Mary* and let it extend into one arm. Bend arm end of wire into a curve. Nestle *Baby Jesus* into curve. Drape metallic-gold, wire-edged ribbon over *Mary*'s head and around *Baby Jesus*, pinning in small tucks with sequin pins pushed into Styrofoam® heads.

Wooden Nativity

Materials:

8" x 10" piece ¾"-thick pine lumber (for crèche and trees)

6" x 8" piece ½"-thick pine lumber (for Mary, Joseph, Baby Jesus, star, and sheep)

Ceramcoat by Delta acrylic paint, colors: Crocus, Tide Pool, Antique Rose, Dunes, Wisteria, Ice Storm, Putty, Black, Deep River

Gel Stain (**Note:** Designer used Home Decor by Delta, color: Fruitwood.)

Dimensional paint, color: black (**Note:** Designer used Tulip fine-line, color: Black Slick.)

Satin varnish (**Note:** Designer used Ceramcoat by Delta.)

½" flat brush

#3 pointed round brush

Stylus

7½" x 24" piece unbleached muslin

Thread to match muslin

One pair black shoelaces

Tracing paper and pencil

Fine-line permanent marking pen, color: black

Sandpaper

Scissors

Ruler

Paper towels

Sewing machine

Scroll saw

1. Transfer crèche and tree patterns onto ¾"-thick pine lumber and remaining patterns onto ½"-thick pine lumber, using tracing paper and pencil. Cut out using scroll saw; sand edges smooth.

2. Paint front surfaces of pieces, using ½" flat brush. Paint as follows: trees—Deep River; star—Crocus; Mary—Antique Rose (**do not** paint face); Joseph—Tide Pool (**do not** paint face); Baby Jesus—Ice Storm (**do not** paint face); and sheep—Putty. Let dry.

3. Paint face and hand areas of Mary, Joseph, and Baby Jesus, using Dunes and #3 pointed brush. Let dry.

4. Paint Mary's hair, Joseph's beard, and sheep faces and ears Black, using #3 pointed brush. Let dry.

5. Paint Baby Jesus' blanket Wisteria. Let dry.

6. When paint is dry, use fine-line permanent marking pen to draw clothing and face outlines, facial features, hair, and sheep's wool squiggles.

7. Make sheep's eyes by first dabbing on small dots of Putty with end of brush. Let dry; then dab on smaller dots of Black atop Putty. Let dry.

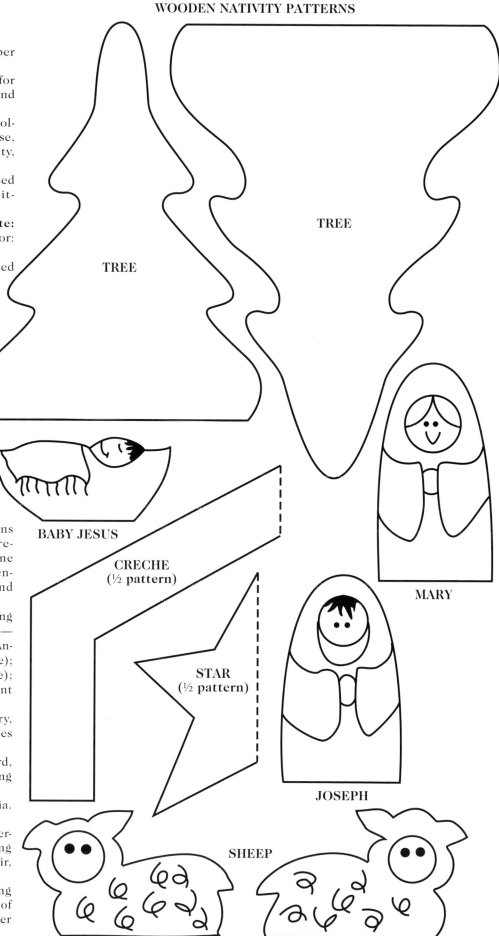

TREE

TREE

BABY JESUS

CRECHE (½ pattern)

STAR (½ pattern)

MARY

JOSEPH

SHEEP

8. Using paper towels and gel stain, apply stain to all surfaces of all pieces, including painted sides.

Note: The unpainted crèche is to be covered entirely with gel stain. Let dry.

9. Apply two coats of varnish to all surfaces of all pieces, letting dry between coats and after second coat.

10. To make bag, fold muslin in half lengthwise, placing right sides of fabric together. Fold down 2½" on end opposite fold. (**Note:** This will be top of bag.) Sew along both 9½" sides, using a ½" seam allowance and leaving a ½" opening 1" down from top fold. Turn bag right-side out and sew two seams around bag, 1" and 1¾" down from top, to form casing.

11. Thread one shoelace through casing, bringing both ends out one side opening. Tie shoelace ends together in a knot.

12. Write *Christ Is Born* on front of bag, using Black Slick dimensional paint. Let dry.

Papier-Mâché Santas

Note: For these projects, a general materials list and instructions have been given. Specific materials and instructions for each project have been listed separately.

General materials:

Paintbrushes: #8 flat, #4 flat, #3 round, #0 liner, ⅜" deerfoot **or** old scruffy brush, 1" sponge
Gesso
Antiquing medium, color: burnt umber
Matte spray finish
Large mixing bowl
Measuring cup
Bowl of warm water
Waxed paper
Paper towels
Wire rack
Airtight container **or** resealable plastic bag
Pencil
Ruler
Scissors
Plastic circle template (helpful for sizing balls)
Sharp knife
Toothpicks
Hot glue gun and glue sticks

General instructions:

1. Cover work surface with waxed paper.

2. Mix needed amount of instant papier-mâché in large mixing bowl, following manufacturer's instructions for mixing. Knead mixture until it has consistency of stiff cookie dough and no dry pieces remain. Add more papier-mâché if mixture is too moist, and sparingly add more water if mixture is too dry. Cover any mixture not being used with waxed paper. Upon completion of project, place excess mixture in airtight container or resealable plastic bag and store in refrigerator.

3. Apply a ⅛"-thick layer of mixture to Styrofoam® cone, using fingers. Moisten hands in bowl of warm water and use fingers to smooth mixture, blending out all bumps and ridges. Let mixture dry; then apply arms, legs, facial features, and texture following instructions for specific project. Keep fingers and modeling tools damp when adding details.

4. Set project on wire rack to dry.

Note: Drying time is usually one–two days. A heater or blow dryer may be used for faster drying.

5. Seal dry piece with even coat of gesso, using sponge paintbrush. Let dry.

6. To paint each piece, use brush size appropriate to area being painted. Apply two coats of paint for base coat, letting paint dry between coats. To apply a wash, thin a small amount of paint with water, thinning to a transparent consistency. Apply paint, deepening shade if desired by adding additional coats of wash, letting paint dry between coats and after final coat. To stipple for highlights or texture, use deerfoot or old scruffy brush. Dip brush in paint, pat on paper towel to remove excess paint, and gently pounce up and down over area to be painted. Let dry thoroughly.

7. To antique piece, thin burnt umber paint with water to make a transparent stain. Apply over surface of project, then wipe quickly and gently with paper towel to remove excess stain.

Note: For best results, apply a light stain and gradually deepen with additional coats if desired, letting dry between coats and after final coat.

8. Lightly mist piece with matte spray finish. Let dry. Glue accessories in place, using hot glue gun.

Santa with Evergreen
Materials:

¼ lb. Celluclay II instant papier-mâché
9" STYROFOAM brand plastic foam cone
Delta Ceramcoat® acrylic paints, colors: burnt umber, tomato spice, light ivory, fleshtone, dark forest, maple sugar, charcoal
DecoArt™ Snow-Tex™ textural medium
2 small silk evergreen sprigs
Miniature pinecone
Red berry
Table knife

1. Follow general instructions to mix papier-mâché and cover cone. Let dry.

2. To make trim on hat, roll a ¾"-thick papier-mâché rope for fur band and a ¾" ball for top of hat. Press rope around cone, placing 2½" from top, and press ball onto top of hat. Blend edges until smooth. Add texture to resemble fur, using toothpick.

3. Form a 1½" papier-mâché ball, flatten, and shape into a beard. Press securely onto face and blend edges until smooth. For hair on each side of head, roll a ¾" x 2½" rope, flatten slightly, and press onto head at an angle from edge of beard to hat trim. Blend edges until smooth. Add texture to beard and hair, using knife.

4. To add papier-mâché facial details, form two ¾" balls and shape into mustache, connecting in center. Press onto face. To make nose, roll a ½" ball and press onto face above mustache. Roll two ½" balls, shape each into an eyebrow, and press onto face. Blend all edges until smooth. Use knife to add texture to mustache and eyebrows. Let papier-mâché dry.

5. Apply coat of gesso and let dry.

6. Apply tomato spice to hat; fleshtone to face; and light ivory to hat trim, hair, beard, eyebrows, and mustache. Paint hat border dark forest with maple sugar trim. Paint light-ivory dots on hat and add ivory-dot flowers with maple sugar, dot centers to hat border. Paint eyes with charcoal and cheeks with tomato-spice wash. Add light-ivory highlights to eyes and cheeks.

7. Follow general instructions to antique, and spray with finish. Let dry.

8. Apply Snow-Tex™ sparingly to head, evergreen sprigs, berry, and pinecone, using finger or end of knife. Let dry. Glue evergreen sprigs, berry, and pinecone to side of hat, referring to photo on page 65 for placement.

Candy-Cane Santa
Materials:

¼ lb. Celluclay II instant papier-mâché
12" STYROFOAM brand plastic foam cone
Delta Ceramcoat® acrylic paints, colors: burnt umber, tomato spice, light ivory, fleshtone, dark forest, maple sugar, charcoal, golden brown, bridgeport, gypsy rose
DecoArt™ Snow-Tex™ textural medium
Table knife

1. Follow general instructions to mix papier-mâché and cover cone. Let dry.

2. To make trim on hat, roll a ½"-thick papier-mâché rope for fur band and a

¾" ball for top of hat. Press rope around cone, placing 1¾" from top, and press ball onto top of hat. Blend edges until smooth. Add texture to resemble fur, using toothpick.

3. Form a 1½" papier-mâché ball, flatten, and shape into a beard. Press securely onto face, placing 1¼" below hat band, and blend edges until smooth. For hair on each side of head, roll a ¾" x 1½" rope, flatten slightly, and press onto head at an angle from edge of beard to hat trim. Blend edges until smooth. Add texture to beard and hair, using knife.

4. To add papier-mâché facial details, form two ½" balls and shape into mustache, connecting in center. Press onto face. To make nose, roll a ⅜" ball and press onto face above mustache. Roll two ¼" balls, shape each into an eyebrow, and press onto face. Blend all edges until smooth. Use knife to add texture to mustache and eyebrows. Make indentation for mouth, using wood end of paintbrush or toothpick. Let papier-mâché dry.

5. For each arm, form a ¾" x 2¾" papier-mâché rope. Press arms onto body, bending slightly and pointing inward. Build up shoulder area with papier-mâché.

6. To add fur trim to coat, roll a ½"-thick papier-mâché rope for coat, two ⅜" x 1¼" ropes for pockets, and two ½"-thick ropes for cuffs. Press ropes firmly in place, referring to photo on page 65 for placement, and blending edges. Add texture to ropes, using toothpick.

7. Apply coat of gesso and let dry.

8. Apply tomato spice to hat and coat; dark forest to mittens; fleshtone to face; and light ivory to hat trim, hair, beard, eyebrows, and mustache. For hat, paint border maple sugar with dark-forest trim. Paint hearts with tomato spice and dots with light ivory. For face, paint eyes with light ivory and let dry. Paint pupils and outline eyes with charcoal. Apply tomato-spice wash to cheeks and mouth. Add light-ivory highlights to eyes and cheeks. For coat, paint button strip dark forest with maple-sugar trim. Paint buttons light ivory with charcoal buttonholes. Paint pockets maple sugar with dark-forest trim, hearts with tomato spice, and teardrop strokes with light ivory. Paint bottom of coat maple sugar with dark-forest stripes, hearts with tomato spice, and teardrop strokes with light ivory. For accessories, paint candy canes light ivory with tomato-spice stripes. Base coat gingerbread man with golden brown; then paint trim

with light ivory, eyes with charcoal, mouth with tomato spice, and bow with dark forest. Base coat mouse with bridgeport and then add tiny, light-ivory dots for muzzle and tips of ears. Paint inside ears and nose gypsy rose with light-ivory highlights. Paint eyes and teeth with light ivory. Add pupils to eyes and outline eyes and teeth with charcoal.

9. Follow general instructions to antique, and spray with finish. Let dry.

10. Apply Snow-Tex™ sparingly to Santa, using finger or end of knife.

Chimney Santa
Materials:
⅓ lb.Celluclay II instant papier-mâché
6" STYROFOAM brand plastic foam cone
5" x 5" x 3" STYROFOAM brand plastic foam block
Delta Ceramcoat® acrylic paints, colors: fleshtone, light ivory, tomato spice, dark forest, maple sugar, red tile, terra cotta, charcoal, burnt umber
DecoArt™ Americana paint, color: slate grey
Duncan Snow Accents
Miniature songsheet
Miniature Christmas gift bag
Miniature Christmas tree
Miniature Christmas wreath
2 miniature candy canes
Miniature French horn
¾" gold liberty bell
Table knife

1. Lay Styrofoam® block on 5" square side. Glue Styrofoam®cone to top center of block, using hot glue gun. Press together to secure, and let set.

2. Follow general instructions to mix papier-mâché and cover figure. Make indentations for bricks while papier-mâché is still moist, using knife. (**Note:** The horizontal mortar lines are ½" apart, the vertical lines are randomly spaced.) Let dry.

Note: When covering chimney, it is best to cover two adjacent sides; let dry; then cover the remaining sides.

3. To make trim on hat, roll a ½"-thick papier-mâché rope for fur band and a ¾" ball for top of hat. Press rope around cone, placing 1½" from top in front, and sloping gradually to 3½" in back. Press ball onto top of hat. Blend edges until smooth. Add texture to resemble fur, using toothpick.

4. To add papier-mâché facial details, form a 1¼" ball, flatten, and shape into a beard. Press onto face so that top of beard adjoins fur trim on hat. Form two

½" balls and shape into mustache, connecting in center. Press onto face. To make nose, roll a ⅜" ball and press onto face above mustache. Shape to form nose. Roll two ¼" balls, shape each into an eyebrow, and press onto face. Blend all edges until smooth. Use knife to add texture to beard, mustache, and eyebrows. Make indentation for mouth, using wood end of paintbrush or toothpick. Let papier-mâché dry.

5. For each arm, form a ¾" x 2¾" papier-mâché rope. Press arms onto body, positioning at base of body. Blend all edges until smooth. Build up shoulder area with papier-mâché. Let papier-mâché dry.

6. To add fur trim to cuffs, roll two ½"-thick papier-mâché ropes and press onto arms. Blend all edges until smooth. Add texture to fur, using toothpick.

7. Apply coat of gesso and let dry.

8. Apply light ivory to beard, mustache, eyebrows, and fur trim. Basecoat face, including mouth, with fleshtone. Paint eyes with light ivory and let dry. Paint pupils and outline eyes with charcoal. Apply tomato-spice wash to cheeks and mouth. Add light-ivory highlights to cheeks. Basecoat hat and coat with tomato spice. Paint dots light ivory. Paint hat border dark forest with maple-sugar trim, dots with maple sugar, and teardrop strokes with light ivory. Paint mittens dark forest. Basecoat top of chimney slate grey. Basecoat bricks red tile; then randomly paint some bricks with a mixture of red tile and terra cotta. Apply slate grey to mortar lines. Stipple slate grey, then charcoal, onto chimney.

9. Follow general instructions to antique, and spray with finish. Let dry.

10. Apply Snow Accents sparingly to Santa, chimney, and songsheet, using finger or end of knife. Let dry. Glue Christmas tree and two candy canes into gift bag. Glue songsheet, liberty bell, gift bag, and French horn atop chimney. Glue wreath to front of chimney.

Celebration Angel

Materials:
225 yds. bedspread thread, white, size 10
Size 8 steel crochet hook
6 cotton balls (for stuffing head)
8½" x 11" piece thin cardboard
Stiffening board (i.e., corrugated cardboard **or** meat tray)
Fabric stiffener
Waxed paper **or** plastic wrap
Rustproof pins

Crochet Abbreviations:
beg—begin(ning)
bet—between
ch—chain stitch
dc—double crochet
dec—decrease
lp(s)—loop(s)
nxt—next
rnd—round
rep—repeat
sc—single crochet
sk—skip
sl st—slip stitch
sp(s)—space(s)
st(s)—stitch(es)
tog—together
tr—treble or triple crochet
yo—yarn over
2 dc shell—2 dc, ch 3, 2 dc
3 dc shell—3 dc, ch 3, 3 dc
3 tr shell—3 tr, ch 3, 3 tr

To finish: Weave beg 1" tail of thread in stitches as you work. Cut end thread 1" long. Pull thread through last stitch and weave through back of stitches. Trim ends.

Head
(Leave a 3" tail to use as marker.) Ch 5, sl st in 1st ch to form ring.
Row 1: Ch 2, make 7 sc in ring (ch 2 counts as 1 sc plus 7 sc—8 sc total). Sl st to ch 2.
Row 2: Ch 2, 2 sc in nxt sc. *Sc in nxt sc, 2 sc in nxt sc.* Rep * rnd—12 sc. (Place marker at end of row.) Sl st in ch 2.
Row 3: Ch 3, 2 dc in nxt sc. *Dc in nxt sc, 2 dc in nxt sc.* Rep * rnd—18 dc. (Move marker.) Sl st in ch 3.
Row 4: Ch 3, 2 dc in nxt dc. *Dc in nxt dc, 2 dc in nxt dc.* Rep * rnd—27 dc. (Move marker.) Sl st in ch 3.
Rows 5–8: Ch 3, dc in each dc rnd—27 dc. Sl st in ch 3. (At end of rows 8, 10, and 17, place cotton balls in head and use blunt end of hook to insert more into neck.)

Chin and Neck
Rows 9 & 10: [To dec: Insert hook in st, yo, pull lp through st—2 lps on hook, insert hook in nxt st, yo, pull lp through st—3 lps on hook, yo, pull thread through all 3 lps.] Ch 2, *dec 1 st, sc in nxt 2 st.* Rep * rnd until you have 20 and 15 sc. Sl st in ch 2.
Row 11: Ch 2, *dec 1 st, sc in nxt st.* Rep * rnd—10 sc. Sl st in ch 2.
Rows 12–14: Ch 2, sc in each sc—10 sc. Sl st in ch 2.

Cape
Row 15: Ch 2, sc in sl st. *2 sc in nxt sc.* Rep * rnd—20 sc. Sl st in ch 2.

Row 16: Ch 2, sc in sl st. *2 sc in nxt sc.* Rep * rnd—40 sc. Sl st in ch 2.
Row 17: Ch 3, dc in each sc—40 dc. Sl st in ch 3.
Rows 18–20: Ch 4, *dc in nxt dc, ch 1.* Rep * rnd—40 dc. Sl st in 3rd ch of ch 4 at beg of row.

Skirt
Row 21: Ch 4, dc in nxt dc. *Ch 1, dc in nxt dc.* Rep * 7 times—10 dc. Sk 10 dc. *Ch 1, dc in nxt dc.* Rep * 9 times—10 dc. Ch 1, sk 10 dc, sl st in 3rd ch.
Row 22: Ch 4, dc in nxt dc. *Ch 1, dc in nxt dc.* Rep * rnd—20 dc. Ch 1, sl st in 3rd ch.
Row 23: Sl st in nxt sp. Ch 3, in same sp make dc, ch 3, 2 dc. *Sk 1 sp, in nxt sp make 2 dc shell.* Rep * rnd—10 shells. Sl st in ch 3, dc in nxt ch-3 sp.
Rows 24–28: Ch 3, dc in same sp, ch 3, 2 dc in same sp. *In nxt sp make 2 dc shell.* Rep * rnd—10 two dc shells. Sl st in ch 3, dc in nxt ch-3 sp.
Rows 29–33: Ch 3, 2 dc in same sp, ch 3, 3 dc in same sp. *In nxt sp make 3 dc shell.* Rep * rnd—10 three dc shells. Sl st in ch 3, dc in nxt ch-3 sp.
Rows 34–37: Ch 4, 2 tr in same sp, ch 3, 3 tr in same sp. *In nxt sp make 3 tr shell.* Rep * rnd—10 three tr shells. Sl st in ch 4, tr in nxt ch-3 sp.
Rows 38 & 39: Ch 4, 2 tr in same sp, ch 3, 3 tr in same sp, ch 1. *In nxt sp make 3 tr shell, ch 1.* Rep * rnd. Sl st in ch 4, tr in nxt ch-3 sp.
Row 40: As Row 38 except instead of ch 1 make ch 2 bet 3 tr shells.
Row 41: As Row 38 except instead of ch 1 make ch 3 bet 3 tr shells.

Skirt Edging
Row 42: Sc in ch-3 sp. Make ch 3, dc in last sc, ch 5, sl st in last dc, ch 8, sl st in same dc, ch 5, sl st in same dc, ch 3, dc in same dc, ch 3, dc in last dc. Sc in center of nxt shell's ch-3 sp.* Rep * rnd except instead of final sc make sl st. Finish.

Sleeves
Row 1: Attach thread in ch-1 sp on Row 21 at underarm. Ch 5, dc in same sp; *sk 1 sp, in nxt sp make dc, ch 3, dc.* Rep * 5 times—7 ch-3 sp, sl st in 3rd ch of ch-5 sp.
Row 2: Ch 5, dc in same sp; *in nxt sp make dc, ch 3, dc.* Rep * 5 times—7 ch-3 sp, sl st in 3rd ch and sp.
Rows 3–8: Ch 3, in same sp make dc, ch 3, 2 dc; *in nxt sp make 2 dc, ch 3, 2 dc.* Rep * 5 times—7 two dc shells, sl st in 3rd ch, dc, and sp.
Rows 9 & 10: Ch 3, in same sp make 2 dc, ch 3, 3 dc; *in nxt sp make 3 dc, ch 3, 3 dc.* Rep * 5 times—7 three dc shells, sl st in 3rd ch, dc, and sp.

Sleeve Edging
Sc in ch-3 sp; *Make ch 3, dc in last sc, ch 5, sl st in last dc, ch 8, sl st in same dc, ch 5, sl st in same dc, ch 3, dc in same dc, sc in nxt sp.* Rep * 6 times except instead of final sc make sl st in 1st sc. Finish.

Wings (make 2)
Row 1: Ch 3, dc in 1st ch. *Ch 3, dc in last dc.* Rep * 10 times—12 sp.
Row 2: Ch 5, sk 1 sp, dc in nxt sp bet dc and ch. *Ch 2, dc in nxt sp bet dc and ch.* Rep * 7 times—9 sp; leaves 2 sp on row 1 for later.
Row 3: Ch 5, turn; in 1st ch-2 sp make 2 dc shell; ch 3, sk nxt sp, sc in nxt sp. *Ch 4, sc in nxt sp.* Rep * 4 times—5 ch-4 sp. Ch 3, in ch-5 sp make 2 dc shell.
Row 4: Ch 5, turn; in ch-3 sp of 2 dc shell make 2 dc shell; ch 3, sc in nxt sp. *Ch 4, sc in nxt sp.* Rep * 4 times. Ch 3, sk ch-3 sp, in ch-3 sp of 2 dc shell make 2 dc shell.
Row 5: Ch 5, turn; in ch-3 sp of 2 dc shell make 2 dc shell; ch 3, sk nxt ch-3 sp, sc in nxt sp. *Ch 4, sc in nxt sp.* Rep * 4 times. Ch 3, in ch-3 sp of 2 dc shell make 2 dc shell.
Rows 6–9: Rep rows 4 & 5 alternately, except on row 9 rep * 3 times instead of 4. Ch 2, sk sp, 2 dc shell in 2 dc shell.
Row 10: Ch 5, turn; 2 dc shell in 2 dc shell, ch 2, sk sp, sc in nxt sp. *Ch 4, sc in nxt sp.* Rep * 2 times. Ch 2, sk sp, 2 dc shell in 2 dc shell.
Row 11: As row 10 except rep * 1 time instead of 2 times.
Row 12: Ch 5, turn; 2 dc shell in 2 dc shell, ch 2, sk sp, sc in nxt sp, ch 4, sc in nxt sp, ch 2, sk sp, 2 dc shell in 2 dc shell.
Row 13: Ch 5, turn; 2 dc shell in 2 dc shell, ch 2, sc in ch-4 sp, ch 2, sk sp, 2 dc in 2 dc shell, ch 2, turn; sc in ch-3 sp of 2 dc shell at beg of this row, ch 1, turn; finish 2 dc shell with 2 dc. Ch 5, turn; sl st in last sc bet top 2 dc shells. Finish.

Wing Edging—Right
Attach thread to sp 12 on row 1. Sc in same sp. *Ch 3, dc in last sc, ch 3, dc in last dc, sc in nxt ch-5 sp.* Rep 1 time. *Make Bow (ch 4, tr in last sc, ch 5, sl st in last tr, ch 8, sl st in same tr, ch 5, sl st in same tr, ch 4, tr in same tr), sc in nxt ch-5 sp.* Rep * 9 times. Ch 4, tr in last sc, sc in 2nd sp; in end sp make Tie (5 sc, ch 5, sl st in last sc, ch 8, sl st in same sc, ch 5, sl st in same sc, 5 sc); sl st in 2nd sp on row 1. Finish.

Wing Edging—Left
Attach thread bet 1st and 2nd sp on row 1 with wing upside down and ch 3

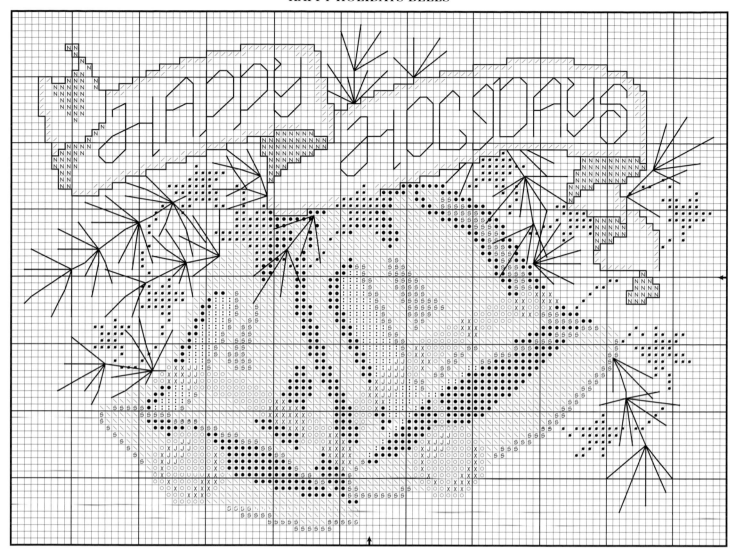

sps to right. In 1st sp make Tie; sc in 2nd sp. Ch 4, tr in last sc, sc in nxt ch 5. *Make Bow, sc in nxt ch-5 sp.* Rep * 9 times. Ch 3, dc in last sc, ch 3, dc in last dc, sc in nxt ch 5; ch 3, dc in last sc, ch 3, dc in last dc, sc in top of 12th sp on row 1. Finish.

Halo

Ch 5, sl st in 1st ch to form ring.
Row 1: Ch 4, in ring; make *dc, ch 1.* Rep * 10 times—12 dc. Sl st in 3rd ch of ch 4.
Row 2: Ch 5, dc in nxt dc, ch 2. *Dc in nxt dc, ch 2.* Rep * 9 times. Sl st in 3rd ch of ch 5.
Row 3: Ch 8, tr in nxt dc, ch 4. *Tr in nxt dc, ch 4.* Rep * 9 times. Sl st in 4th ch of ch 8.
Row 4: Ch 2, *in nxt sp make 5 sc, sc in tr.* Rep * rnd ending with 5 sc, sl st in ch 2.
Row 5: Ch 2, sc in each sc. Sl st in ch 2. Finish.
To stiffen: Make a cone from cardboard. Tape to hold shape. Cover with waxed paper or plastic wrap. Saturate all but head of angel in fabric stiffener or a 2-to-1 solution of fresh white glue and water. Gently squeeze out excess. Insert cone in skirt. Shape skirt, arms, and shoulders. Pin wings on waxed-paper-covered stiffening board. Leave until almost dry. Remove pins and cone. Shape arms up and out. Adjust skirt so angel stands. Let dry completely. Squeeze angel head to shape desired. Sew halo to back of head. Tack wings together at center and each end. Tack tips of first bow to halo. Tack wings to skirt. Dab glue on stitch points. Let dry. Trim threads. Curve wings back. Reshape head as desired.

Happy Holidays Bells

DMC	DMC Metallic	Color
● 814		garnet, dk.
\ 321		red
S 3705		melon, dk.
: 3706		melon, med.
X 783		gold
o 444		lemon, dk.
J 445		lemon, lt.
N 825		blue, dk.
/ 813		blue, lt.
•⌐ 307		lemon
	284	gold
bs 828		blue, ul. lt.
ss 701		green, lt.

Fabric: 14-count black Aida from Charles Craft, Inc.
Stitch count: 76H x 103W
Design size:

11-count	7" x 9⅜"
14-count	5½" x 7⅜"
18-count	4¼" x 5¾"
22-count	3½" x 4⅝"

Instructions: Cross stitch using two strands of floss. Backstitch (bs) using two strands of floss. Straight stitch (ss) using three strands of floss.

Backstitch (bs) instructions:
828   outer edge of banner
3705   lettering
Straight stitch (ss) instructions:
701   greenery

TOP

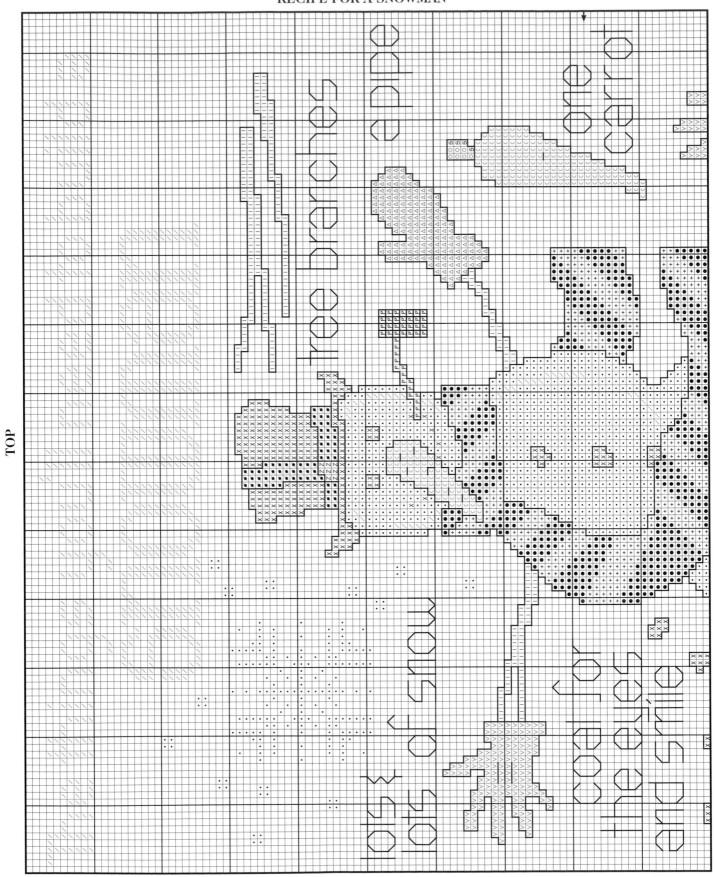

Shaded portion indicates overlap from previous page.

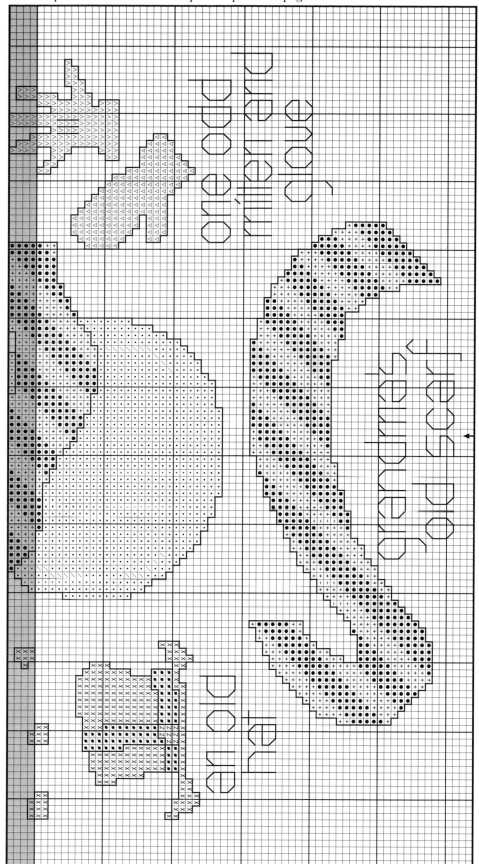

Recipe for a Snowman

	Anchor	DMC	Color
╱	117	341	blue violet, lt.
X	403	310	black
I	370	434	brown, lt.
+	44	815	garnet, med.
●	899	3782	mocha brown, lt.
V	391	3033	mocha, vy. lt.
Z	235	414	steel gray, dk.
✂	400	317	pewter gray
P	307	783	gold
△	127	823	navy, dk.
C	313	742	tangerine, lt.
○	230	909	emerald, vy. dk.
S	923	699	green
•	1	white	white
bs	316	970	pumpkin, lt.
bs	903	3032	mocha, med.
bs	371	400	mahogany, dk.

Fabric: 28-count pastel blue linen from Zweigart®
Stitch count: 160H x 123W
Design size:

14-count	11½" x 8⅞"
18-count	8⅞" x 6⅞"
28-count	11½" x 8⅞"
32-count	10" x 7¾"

Instructions: Cross stitch over two threads, using two strands of floss. Backstitch (bs) using one strand of floss.

Backstitch (bs) instructions:

117	341	snowman
371	400	branches, pipe
316	970	carrots
230	909	carrot top
903	3032	gloves
403	310	eyes, coal, buttons
400	317	scarves, mittens, hats, lettering

Starry Christmas Quilt

Materials:

- ½ yd. 44/45"-wide periwinkle blue floral-print fabric (for border and piecing)
- ⅓ yd. 44/45"-wide periwinkle blue solid fabric (for border and piecing)
- ⅓ yd. 44/45"-wide yellow solid fabric (for border and piecing)
- ¼ yd. **each** 44/45"-wide print fabrics, colors: rose, multicolor floral, two **different** blues
- ½ yd. 44/45"-wide dark green print fabric (for binding and piecing)
- 1 yd. 44/45"-wide complementary fabric, cut 36" square (for backing)
- 36" square lightweight quilt batting
- Thread to match fabrics (for piecing)

Quilting thread, color: periwinkle blue
Hand-sewing and quilting needles
Straight pins
¼"-wide masking tape
Plastic (for templates)
Mechanical pencil
Scissors
Ruler
Iron
Sewing machine (optional)

Finished size: 32" x 32"
Note: Please read all instructions carefully before beginning. Use a ¼" seam allowance throughout. Pattern pieces **do not** include seam allowance. Use 100% cotton fabrics.

1. Trace around all pattern pieces on plastic to make templates. Cut out.
2. To conserve fabric, cut borders first. Cut four 1" x 36" strips from yellow solid. Cut four 1½" x 36" strips from periwinkle blue solid. Cut four 3" x 36" strips from periwinkle blue floral.
3. Draw around each template on wrong side of fabric as follows, using mechanical pencil for a narrow line and leaving at least ½" space between each piece to allow for ¼" seam allowance. Cut out.
   Template A: Cut two from multicolor floral and two from periwinkle blue floral.
   Template B: Cut eight **each** from yellow solid, rose print, periwinkle blue solid, and one blue print, for a total of thirty-two large triangles.
   Template C: Cut sixteen **each** from second blue print, rose print, dark green print, and yellow solid, for a total of sixty-four small triangles.
Note: Be careful to place long side of triangle (Template C) on straight grain of fabric.
4. There are two block colorations in this quilt. To piece first block coloration, join rose print and periwinkle blue solid large triangles (Template B) to make eight units. Join two yellow solid, one dark green print, and one blue print small triangles (Template C) to make eight units. Assemble star as follows, referring to photo on page **72** for color placement.

STARRY CHRISTMAS QUILT TEMPLATES

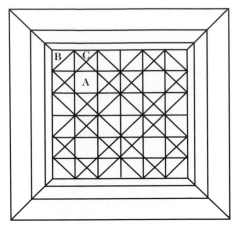

STARRY CHRISTMAS QUILT SCHEMATIC

Row 1: Rose print/periwinkle blue solid unit, yellow solid/green print/blue print unit, rose print/periwinkle blue solid unit.
Row 2: Yellow solid/green print/blue print unit, multicolor floral square (Template A), yellow solid/green print/blue print unit.
Row 3: Repeat Row 1, referring to photo for color placement.
Repeat for second star.
5. To piece second block coloration, join yellow and first blue print large triangles (Template B) to make eight units. Join two rose print, one dark green print, and one second blue print small triangles (Template C) to make eight units. Assemble star as follows, referring to photo for color placement.

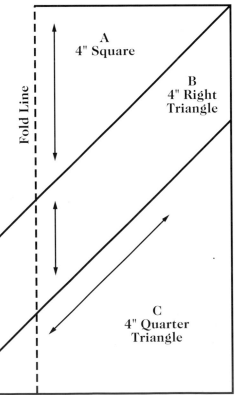

Row 1: Yellow solid/first blue print unit, rose print/second blue print/green print unit, yellow solid/first blue print unit.
Row 2: Rose print/first blue print/green print unit, periwinkle blue floral (Template A), rose print/first blue print/green print unit.
Row 3: Repeat Row 1, referring to photo for color placement.
Repeat for second star.
6. Join four completed blocks to form quilt top, referring to photo for block placement. Make border by sewing yellow solid, periwinkle blue solid, and periwinkle blue floral border strips together. Repeat to make four borders. Join borders to four sides of quilt top, mitering corners as you go. Press completed quilt top.
7. Place backing fabric right-side down atop a flat surface. Place batting atop backing fabric and completed quilt top right-side up atop batting. Pin and baste through all layers.
8. To quilt, take small running stitches through all three layers, using a small needle. Quilt diagonal lines corner to corner through all four blocks. Outline quilt small yellow solid and rose-print triangles to emphasize star design, using ¼" masking tape as a guide. Hand or machine quilt in the ditch along all three borders. Remove pins.
9. To make binding, cut dark green fabric into four 2" x 44" strips. Piece strips together to form one long strip. Fold in half along lengthwise edge, and pin around perimeter of quilt front, aligning raw edges. Sew binding to quilt. Remove pins. Turn binding to back of quilt and blind stitch in place.
10. Be sure to sign the back of your quilt with either a permanent pen or in stitches. If you wish to hang your quilt for display, add a sleeve for a dowel or attach a curtain ring for hanging at each top corner.

I'll Be Home for Christmas Quilt

Materials:
⅛ yd. **each** 44/45"-wide print fabrics, colors: dark green, red, gray, light beige, black, light blue
⅓ yd. 44/45"-wide white fabric
⅛ yd. 44/45"-wide small tan-print fabric
⅓ yd. 44/45"-wide dark-green-solid fabric
¼ yd. 44/45"-wide red-solid fabric
¼ yd. 44/45"-wide floral-print fabric in Christmas colors

1 yd. 44/45"-wide complementary fabric, cut 28" square (for backing)
28" square lightweight quilt batting
8" length ⅛"-wide red satin ribbon (for wreath on door)
8" length ¼"-wide green grosgrain ribbon (for wreath on door)
Thread to match fabrics (for piecing)
Quilting thread, colors: white, green
Plastic (for templates)
Mechanical pencil
Silver marking pencil (for marking quilting designs)
¼"-wide masking tape (for marking quilting designs)
Hand-sewing and quilting needles
Straight pins
Scissors
Iron
Permanent fine-line marker (optional)
Clear nylon monofilament machine-quilting thread (optional)
Sewing machine (optional)

Note: Please read all instructions carefully before beginning. Use a ¼" seam allowance throughout. Pattern pieces **do not** include seam allowance.

1. Trace around all pattern pieces on plastic to make templates. Cut out.
2. Draw around each template on wrong side of fabric as follows, using mechanical pencil for a narrow line and leaving at least ½" space between each piece to allow for ¼" seam allowance. Cut out.
   Template A: Cut one from dark green print.
   Template B: Cut two from red print, two from gray print, and one from light beige print.
   Template C: Cut one from light beige print and one from gray print.
   Template D: Cut one from red print.
   Template E: Cut one from black print.
   Template F: Cut one from light blue print, turn template over, and cut one in reverse from light blue print.
   Template G: Cut two from red print.
   Template H: Cut one from light blue print.
   Template I: Cut one from light blue print.

3. To piece house block, join red print, beige print, red print, and gray print (Template B) together. Join light beige print and gray print (Template C) together and add to assembled Template B pieces. Finish the row with one gray print (Template B) piece. Join to dark green print (Template A).
4. Join red print (Template D) to black print (Template E) to form roof. Join one red print (Template G) to either side of light blue print (Template H) to form chimneys. Join chimney section to roof section.
5. Join light blue print (Template F) to either side of roof section. Be careful to sew only to the point where G, E, D, and F meet. **Do not** sew into the seam allowance.
6. Join light blue print (Template I) to top of house block and press block gently with iron.
7. Cut two 9⅜" squares from white fabric. Cut these squares in half on the diagonal, forming four triangles. Join these four triangles to the house block.
8. For log-cabin sections, cut the following pieces. Cut one 5½" square from small tan print. Cut this square in half on both diagonals to form four triangles. Cut two 2" x 44" strips **each** from dark green solid and red solid and three 2" x 44" strips from floral print.
9. To make log-cabin sections, sew one dark green strip to small tan triangle, beginning at 90°-angle corner. Press strip away from triangle and trim end of strip even with 90°-angle end of triangle. Sew dark green strip to second side of

tan triangle, beginning where first green strip starts. Press strip away from triangle and trim end of strip even with 90°-angle end of triangle. Repeat with red strips and floral strips. Be careful not to stretch pieces while sewing or pressing: the bias edge stretches easily. Repeat these steps to make four log-cabin corner sections.
10. Join four corner sections to white triangles surrounding house block. Press finished top lightly with iron.
11. Use silver pencil to mark quilting design in large, white triangles.
12. Place backing fabric right-side down atop a flat surface. Place batting atop backing fabric and completed quilt top right-side up atop batting. Pin and baste through all layers.
13. To hand quilt, take small running stitches through all three layers, using a small quilting needle. Use green quilting thread on Template-A piece,

QUILTING PATTERN

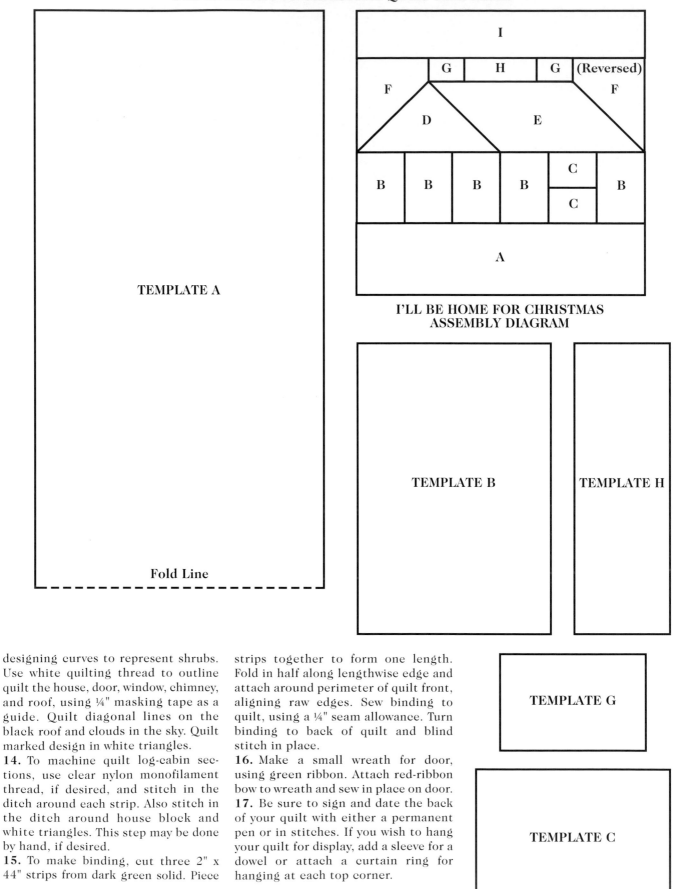

TEMPLATE A

Fold Line

I

G   H   G   (Reversed)

F   F

D   E

B   B   B   B   C   B
            C

A

**I'LL BE HOME FOR CHRISTMAS
ASSEMBLY DIAGRAM**

TEMPLATE B

TEMPLATE H

TEMPLATE G

TEMPLATE C

designing curves to represent shrubs. Use white quilting thread to outline quilt the house, door, window, chimney, and roof, using ¼" masking tape as a guide. Quilt diagonal lines on the black roof and clouds in the sky. Quilt marked design in white triangles.

14. To machine quilt log-cabin sections, use clear nylon monofilament thread, if desired, and stitch in the ditch around each strip. Also stitch in the ditch around house block and white triangles. This step may be done by hand, if desired.

15. To make binding, cut three 2" x 44" strips from dark green solid. Piece strips together to form one length. Fold in half along lengthwise edge and attach around perimeter of quilt front, aligning raw edges. Sew binding to quilt, using a ¼" seam allowance. Turn binding to back of quilt and blind stitch in place.

16. Make a small wreath for door, using green ribbon. Attach red-ribbon bow to wreath and sew in place on door.

17. Be sure to sign and date the back of your quilt with either a permanent pen or in stitches. If you wish to hang your quilt for display, add a sleeve for a dowel or attach a curtain ring for hanging at each top corner.

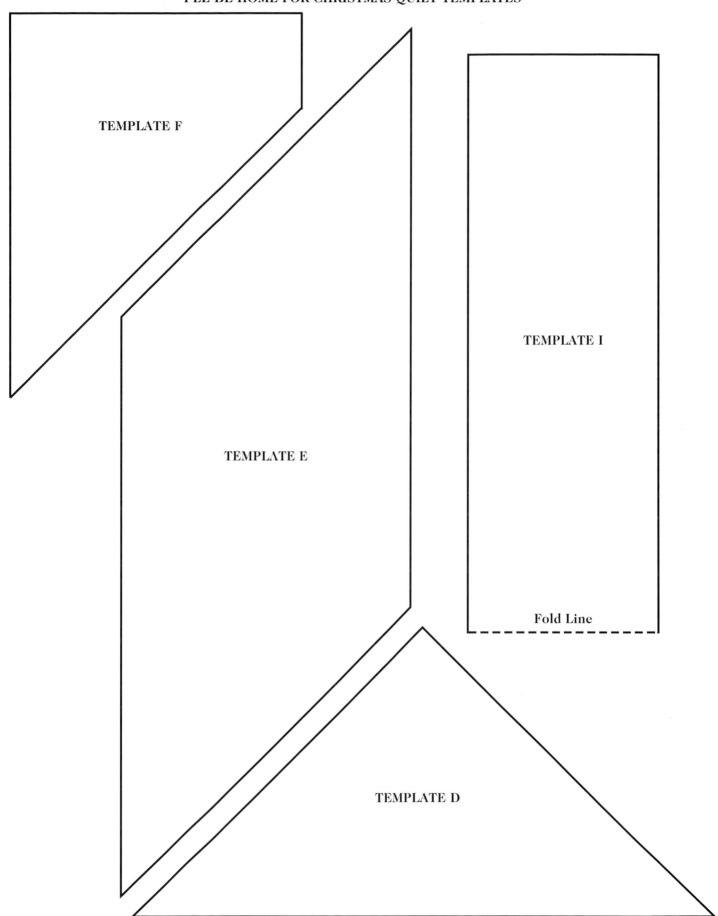

TEMPLATE F

TEMPLATE I

TEMPLATE E

Fold Line

TEMPLATE D

Floral Zigzag Rug

Crochet Abbreviations and Terms:
bet—between
ch—chain stitch
dc—double crochet
lp(s)—loop(s)
nxt—next
rem—remaining
rep—repeat
RS—right side
sc—single crochet
sc dec—single crochet decrease: (Draw up lp in nxt st) twice, yo, draw through 3 lps on hook.
sl st—slip stitch
sp—space
st(s)—stitch(es)
yo—yarn over

Materials:
Caron Wintuk 4-ply Hand Knitting Yarn, 100% Orlon, 3.5-oz. skein, colors: No. 65 winter white (6 skeins); No. 36 spruce; No. 31 cardinal red
Size N crochet hook, **or** size needed to obtain gauge
Tapestry needle

Gauge: Over sc 5 sts = 3"
Finished size: 32" x 17½"

Note: Work rug using four strands of yarn held together.

Center
With white, ch 51.
Row 1 (RS): Sc in 2nd ch from hook; sc in each rem ch across, turn—50 sts.
Row 2: Ch 1, sc in each st across; turn.

Rows 3–8: Rep Row 2.
Row 9: Ch 1, sc in first st, sc dec, sc across to within last 3 sts, sc dec, sc in last st; turn—48 sts.
Rows 10–12: Ch 1; work even, turn.
Row 13: Rep Row 9—46 sts.
Rows 14–16: Ch 1; work even, turn.
Row 17: Rep Row 9—44 sts.
Row 18: Ch 1; work even, turn.
Row 19: Rep Row 9—42 sts.
Row 20: Ch 1; work even, turn.
Row 21: Do not ch; sl st in first st, sc dec, sc to within last 3 sts, sc dec, turn (1 st remains unworked at end of row)—38 sts.
Row 22: Ch 1; work even, turn.
Rows 23–26: Rep Rows 21 and 22 alternately—30 sts at end of Row 26.
Rows 27–31: Rep Row 21—10 sts. Fasten off.

Embroidery
1. Work motif from Illustration 1 over Rows 5–8, working from A to B five times, then from A to C once, having 3 sts bet each edge of rug and motifs.
2. Work motif from Illustration 2 over Rows 15–18, repeating from A to B three times, then from A to C once, having peaks of motifs over valleys of previous row of motifs.
3. Work motif from Illustration 1 over Rows 25–28, repeating from A to B once, and from A to C once, having peaks of motifs over valleys of previous row of motifs.

Border
Row 1: With right sides facing, join white at beg of Row 1 of *Center*. Work 90 sc evenly spaced along curved edge, ending at straight edge; turn.

Row 2: Ch 1, sc in each st of Row 1 of *Border;* turn.
Row 3: Ch 1, sc in each st of Row 2 of *Border.* Fasten off.

Embroidery
Work running stitch using red at base of Row 2 of *Border.* Work running stitch using green at base of Row 3 of *Border.*

Log-Cabin Wreath

Materials:
One 14" x 11" sheet 10-mesh plastic canvas
Needloft plastic-canvas yarn, colors: eggshell #39 (8 yds.), beige #40 (7½ yds.), white #41 (6 yds.), Christmas red #2 (9½ yds.), fern #23 (4 yds.), mint #24 (5 yds.), Christmas green #28 (4 yds.)
#16 tapestry needle
Tacky glue
Scissors
Purchased frame of your choice

Finished size: 9" x 9" (excluding bow)
Note: Yarn measurements given are pre-split. If using whole yarn in appropriate size for 10-mesh plastic canvas, double required yardage.

1. Split all yarn before stitching.
2. Cut one 101-thread square from plastic canvas for wreath. Stitch wreath design centered on plastic-canvas square, following color numbers indicated on chart on page **101** and using gobelin stitch.
3. To make bow, cut two 17 x 54-thread pieces for loops, one 5 x 23-thread

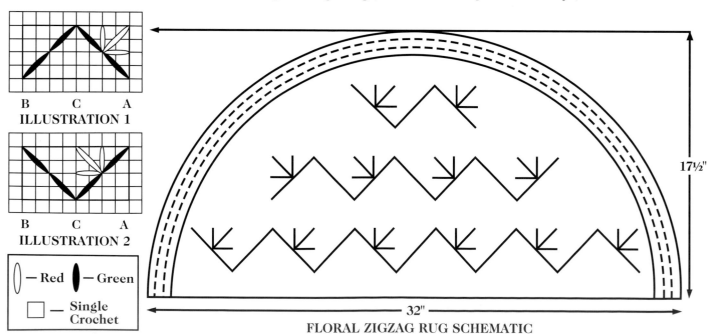

B   C   A
ILLUSTRATION 1

B   C   A
ILLUSTRATION 2

⬭ — Red   ⬬ — Green
▢ — Single Crochet

FLORAL ZIGZAG RUG SCHEMATIC

32"

17½"

LOG-CABIN WREATH

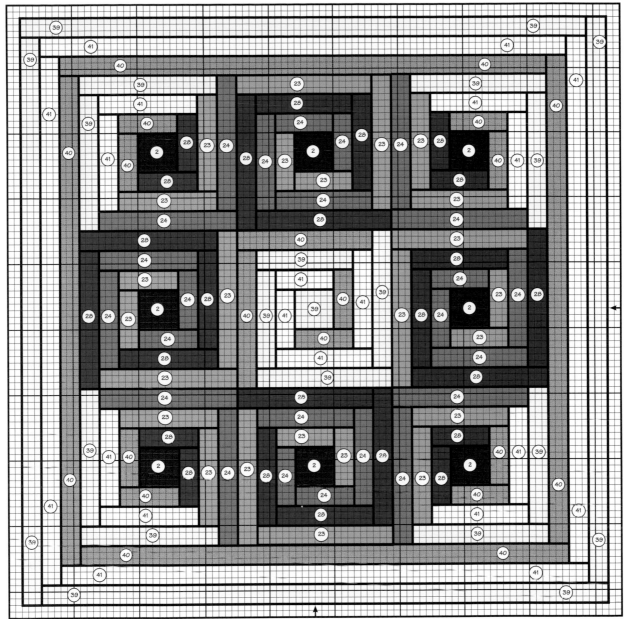

piece for center strip, and two 17 x 40-thread pieces for streamers. Work gobelin stitches to cover each bow piece, using red yarn. Carefully trim away excess canvas, using scissors and following outline of stitched design. (**Note:** Refer to heavy, dark outline on chart.) Overcast edges of each bow piece, using beige yarn.

4. To assemble bow, shape each loop piece into a loop and tack ends together. Whipstitch loops together at center. Wrap center strip around center of bow and whipstitch ends together in back. Tack top-right corner of one streamer to top-left corner of remaining streamer. Tack tops of streamers to center back of bow.

5. Frame wreath as desired. Glue bow to center bottom of wreath, referring to photo on page **68** for placement.

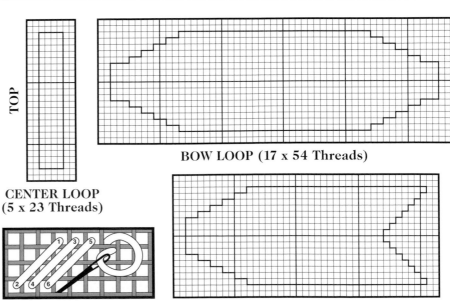

TOP

CENTER LOOP
(5 x 23 Threads)

BOW LOOP (17 x 54 Threads)

GOBELIN STITCH

STREAMER (17 x 40 Threads)

GIFTS TO TREASURE

Gift-giving provides us with wonderful opportunities to express our creativity; and the recipients of our handiwork are certain to have a special fondness for these treasures from our hands. Included on the following pages is a collection of gift ideas for Christmas lovers of all ages. The added beauty of these projects is that many of them, such as the Children Around the World and Painted Photo Frames, will be ideal for children to make and give—and that means that you can include your little ones in the preparations for the season ahead in a way they're guaranteed to love! And while their little hands are busy creating their holiday wonders, you can work on your own projects, such as the adorable Festive Felt Snowman, the colorful Quilted Coasters, or the beautiful Broomstick-Lace Afghan.

To: Mom
From: Cole

Seasonal Pleasers

We believe that gift-giving is the very best part of Christmas. And when the gifts are hand-made, they are especially admired by their lucky recipients, because they are a treasure from both the hands and the heart. While purchased gifts are nice, we have found that the objects we have created by hand with someone in mind are the pieces that are prized the most. And so, each year, we spend the months leading up to the Christmas season searching for ideas for wonderful presents for all the special people on our gift list, digging through our stash of handiworking supplies, and shopping when necessary to find the materials we will need to create Christmas pleasers that will be cherished for years to come.

Above—Everyone wants her entire home to reflect the spirit of the season, and we think these **Christmas Hand Towels** *are the ideal yuletide accessories for the powder room. Cross-stitched on fingertip towels, these designs will help make your holidays merry and bright. One bears the message, "Merry Christmas to all who may dwell here," and displays a quaint little cottage with a picket fence and a wreath on the front door. The second towel is an innovative treatment of the word JOY. The J and Y are red candles, with flames topping them; and the O is a wreath of greenery decorated with a ribbon bow and French-knot holly berries. Charts are on page 118.*

Above—*His arms stretched open wide, this chubby snowman practically begs for a hug. A snazzy plaid scarf keeps his snowy neck toasty on cold, winter nights. Shiny black buttons serve as his eyes and mouth, and two large buttons dress up his snow "suit." Children will love this floppy, cuddly friend, but be sure to sew the buttons on very securely if your snowman will be used as a toy. Place "Frosty" under your tree with the piles of packages or seat him on the sofa among Christmas pillows and warm afghans. We know you have the perfect place for this* **Festive Felt Snowman** *in your house! Instructions begin on page 115.*

Above—*Just right for cool winter evenings, this* **Broomstick-Lace Afghan** *gets its name in an unusual way—you place the beginning crochet stitches on a knit pin that is about the size of a broomstick. You can actually use a broomstick if you wish! A fun-to-stitch crochet project, the lacy-looking afghan will enhance any room of your house. Use it as a lap throw, drape it over a chair, or cuddle down for a long winter's nap beneath it—its comforting warmth will make it a permanent fixture in your home for years to come. Instructions are on page 114.*

106

Above—Even if you have never quilted before, you can make these **Quilted Coasters**. *Each star design is made from simple, geometric shapes, pieced together by machine or by hand, and then quilted with metallic thread. This set is a wonderful way to use those bits of Christmas fabric you have been saving in a scrap bag. We chose red, white, and green solids and a light floral print for our fast-and-easy coasters; and we were able to make several sets in a short amount of time—what more could you ask of a holiday project? Instructions begin on page 114.*

Above—*Remember making paper snowflakes by folding white paper and cutting shapes into it? The surprise and pleasure at each new creation was one of the many small joys of childhood. This project involves the same technique on a more sophisticated level. You'll trace and cut out our pattern; and when you unfold your paper, you'll find a circle of children holding hands around a center snowflake. Mat your* **Children Around the World** *on a solid-color background, frame, and you'll have a unique wall decoration to give or to keep. Instructions begin on page 121.*

Above—Add a personal touch to a pair of clear acrylic photo frames with paint—what clever quick-and-easy gifts! Paint red apples and letters of the alphabet for a special teacher or Christmas bulbs for a holiday-loving friend. They will be touched by your thoughtfulness and will enjoy adding their own photos to these **Painted Photo Frames**. Instructions begin on page 120.

Right—Christmas mail is fun to get, especially from family members and friends we have not heard from for a while! We always enjoy keeping cards and letters and poring over them after the holidays are long gone. This gives us a chance to update our address books and enjoy the pictures and personal messages. The handsome **Mail Holder** is easy to make and will be the choice spot for Christmas greetings. Instructions are on page 120.

109

Right—This cross-stitch vision of sugarplums comes complete with lollipop trees, gumdrop shrubs, and a smiling gingerbread man in the front yard. His gingerbread residence has a peppermint-candy decoration hung above the front door and a delectable-looking icing roof with colorful sprinkles. Christmas-tree cookies stand beside the house, also decorated with candy ornaments. A gingerbread house is truly a holiday tradition; and this darling cross-stitch design, titled **Gingerbread House**, will make a charming addition to anyone's kitchen, where tasty, edible gingerbread men and houses are being concocted, or anywhere else in a Christmastime home. Chart is on page 119.

Left—With a few simple seams, a basic doily can be quickly transformed into a decorative pillow. If you don't want to use old doilies inherited from your mother or grandmothers, look for new ones at your local department store. This pair of **Doily Pillows** will make a great Christmas gift for a soon-to-be bride. Before they are put to decorative use in her new home, they can be carried down the aisle during her wedding by two ring bearers! Instructions begin on page 119.

Above—*Ready-to-cover metal button forms have a brand-new use! Customize your sweaters and blouses with our* **House Buttons** *cross-stitch designs that you stitch on Aida cloth and use to cover button forms. Manufactured in several sizes, the button forms are available in most fabric and craft stores. We have chosen three colorful, tiny houses to use in changing the look of this sweater from ordinary to eye-catching! Charts are on page 120.*

111

Above—Transform plastic canvas into works of art with metallic ribbon and beads. You'll be using cross-stitching skills on quick-and-easy plastic canvas, and the results will be these spectacular **Ribbon and Bead Package Tags**. *These three gold, red, and green ornaments have a rich look that will give your Christmas packages extra flair and appeal. You'll also learn two stitches that may be new to you but will surely come in handy in the future—the Smyrna cross stitch and the slanting Gobelin stitch, which are both clearly illustrated in the instructions. These sparkling, holiday "gems" can also be used as ornaments—a nifty trick is to make two of each and whipstitch them together to make these branch trimmers reversible. No matter which way they hang, they'll be putting their best side forward. Charts begin on page 124.*

Right—Make your kitchen aromatic during the holidays when you craft this charming **Apple and Cinnamon Tree** wall hanging. The tree section is made from dried apple slices, with attached red-ribbon bows and jingle bells. Cinnamon sticks form the trunk; their spicy scent will please you throughout the season. Instructions are on page 123.

Left—If you've never tried papier tole, this **Papier Tole Snowman** will give you a great introduction! You'll use paper silhouettes, painted, stacked, and glued together to give depth to the snowman. Place this whimsical character inside a twig wreath, attach it to a velvet ribbon for hanging purposes, or top it with a perky plaid bow, and you'll have a fun and festive snowman to hang on a wall or door in your home. Instructions begin on page 122.

Broomstick-Lace Afghan

Crochet Abbreviations:
bet—between
ch—chain stitch
lp(s)—loop(s)
nxt—next
rep—repeat
sc—single crochet
sl st—slip stitch
st(s)—stitch(es)
yo—yarn over

Materials:
Thirteen 3½-oz. skeins J. & P. Coats 4-ply
   hand-knitting yarn, 100% acrylic,
   color: 111 natural
Size 50 knit pin **or** broomstick
Size J crochet hook

Finished size: 68" x 112"

Step 1: Ch 200. Place lp at end of chain on knit pin, holding pin in left hand and working from left to right, *insert hook through nxt ch, yo, pull yarn through and place lp on knit pin. Rep from * until 200 sts (lps) are on knit pin. **Do not turn.**

Step 2: **Slide five lps from knit pin, turn lps counter-clockwise to form one large lp, and work 5 sc in lp. Rep from ** to end of row. **Do not turn.**

Note: For step 2, designer removed all lps from knit pin at one time. If using this method, be careful not to pull out any of the lps.

Step 3: Place lp from last sc on knit pin, ***working from right to left, insert hook around next sc, yo, pull yarn through to create lp, and place on knit pin. Repeat from *** until 200 sts are on knit pin.

Note: Steps 2 and 3 make one pattern row. Repeat to make a total of 69 lp rows, ending after step 2. **Do not fasten off.**

Edging Row: Work 1 sc in last large lp made, then down side edge, work 2 sc in same lp; *1 sc in side of nxt Step 2 row, 2 sc in nxt lp; rep from * to corner large lp; work 7 sc in lp, **1 sc bet lps, 5 sc in nxt lp; rep from **, working 7 sc in last corner lp; rep from * to corner; sl st to top of first sc of last Step 2 row.

Quilted Coasters

Materials:
¼ yd. 44/45"-wide red-and-green floral print with ivory background fabric
⅛ yd. 44/45"-wide white-on-white print fabric
⅛ yd. 44/45"-wide red-print fabric
⅛ yd. 44/45"-wide dark green with white pindots fabric
Four 4½" squares lightweight cotton batting
Thread to match fabrics
Metallic-gold thread (for quilting)
Plastic (for templates)
Mechanical pencil
Straight pins
Scissors
Transparent ruler
Hand-sewing needles **and** quilting needles
Iron
Rotary cutter and cutting mat (optional)
Sewing machine (optional)

Finished size: 4" x 4"
Note: Materials listed will make four *Quilted Coasters.* Please read all instructions carefully before beginning. Use a ¼" seam allowance throughout. Pattern pieces **do not** include seam allowance. Use 100% cotton fabrics.

1. Trace around all pattern pieces on plastic to make templates. Cut out.
2. To conserve fabric, cut borders and backing squares first. For borders, cut four 1" x 3½" strips **each** from red print and dark green with white pindots. Cut four 1" x 4½" strips **each** from red print and dark green with white pindots. For backing squares, cut four 4½" squares from red-and-green floral print.
3. Draw around **each** template on wrong side of fabric as follows, using mechanical pencil for a narrow line and leaving at least ½" space between **each** piece to allow for a ¼" seam allowance. Cut out.
   Template A: Cut eight from white-on-white print and four from red print.
   Template B: Cut twelve **each** from dark green with white pindots and

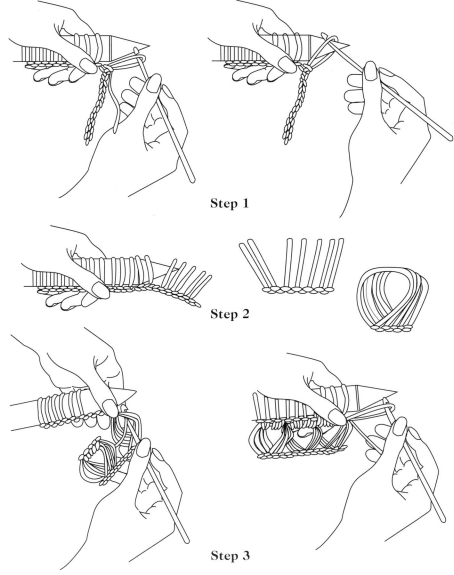

Step 1

Step 2

Step 3

BROOMSTICK-LACE AFGHAN ILLUSTRATIONS

white-on-white print. Cut four from red-and-green floral print.
Template C: Cut four **each** from white-on-white print and red-and-green floral print.
Template D: Cut eight from white-on-white print, twelve from red-and-green floral print, and four from dark green with white pindots.

4. To assemble squares for coaster blocks, refer to Assembly Guide and join units as follows:
Square 1: Join white-on-white and dark green with white pindots triangles (Template B) to make eight squares.
Square 2: Join white-on-white and red-and-green floral-print triangles (Template B) to make four squares.
Square 3: Join white-on-white and red-and-green floral-print rectangles (Template C) to make four squares.
Square 4: Join white-on-white and red-and-green floral-print triangles (Template D) to make four half-squares. Join dark green with white pindots and red-and-green floral-print triangles (Template D) to make four half-squares. Join white/floral print half-squares and green/floral print half-squares to make four squares.
Square 5: Join white-on-white and red-and-green floral-print triangles (Template D) to make four half-squares. Join half-squares and dark green with white pindots triangles (Template B) to make four squares.

5. To assemble each coaster block, follow the Assembly Guide and join squares together to make three rows of three squares each. Refer to photo on page **107** for square placement. Join rows together to make block. Press seam allowances toward darker-color fabrics.
6. Sew a 1" x 3½" border strip to side edges of each coaster block, referring to photo for placement. Sew a 1" x 4½" border strip to top and bottom edges of each coaster block. Press seam allowances toward border strips.
7. For each coaster, place batting square atop a flat surface. Place backing square right-side up atop batting and pieced front right-side down atop backing square, aligning raw edges. Pin layers together. Sew together around edges, leaving a 1½" opening for turning. Remove pins. Clip corners, turn right-side out, and whipstitch opening closed.
8. Hand or machine quilt in the ditch along borders on each block, using metallic-gold thread.

Festive Felt Snowman

Materials:
12" x 40" piece white felt
4" square orange felt
12" x 18" piece black felt
3" strip 44/45"-wide plaid fabric of your choice
Thread, colors: white, black, orange, color to match plaid fabric
Two ½" black ball-type buttons
Three ¼" black ball-type buttons
Two 1⅛" black flat buttons
Polyester filling
Folk Art Acrylic Paint, color: #930 primrose (for blush)
Stiff bristle brush, size: medium
Measuring tape
Hand-sewing needle
Straight pins
Tissue paper
Pencil
Ruler
Scissors
Iron

Finished size: 13" tall
Note: Use a ¼" seam allowance throughout. Because of the stretching quality of felt when it is stuffed, pattern pieces do not show placement of facial features. The instructions include placement of facial features as used in the model. It may be necessary to adjust measurements for proper placement on your snowman, depending on size difference after stuffing.

1. Transfer patterns to tissue paper. Cut out.
2. Cut two head and body pieces, four hand and arm pieces, and four foot and leg pieces from white felt.
3. To assemble hands and arms, place two hand and arm pieces with right sides together, aligning raw edges. Sew together, leaving short, straight edge unstitched. Clip curve between thumb and fingers. Trim edges close to seam. Turn right-side out. Stuff firmly with polyester filling to within ⅜" of opening. Baste opening closed. Repeat with remaining hand and arm pieces. Set aside.

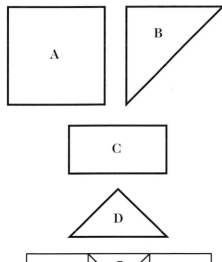

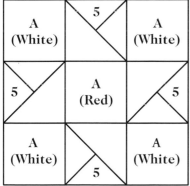

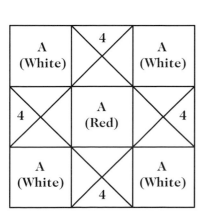

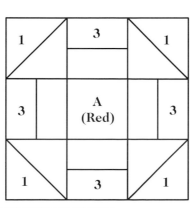

QUILTED COASTERS ASSEMBLY GUIDE

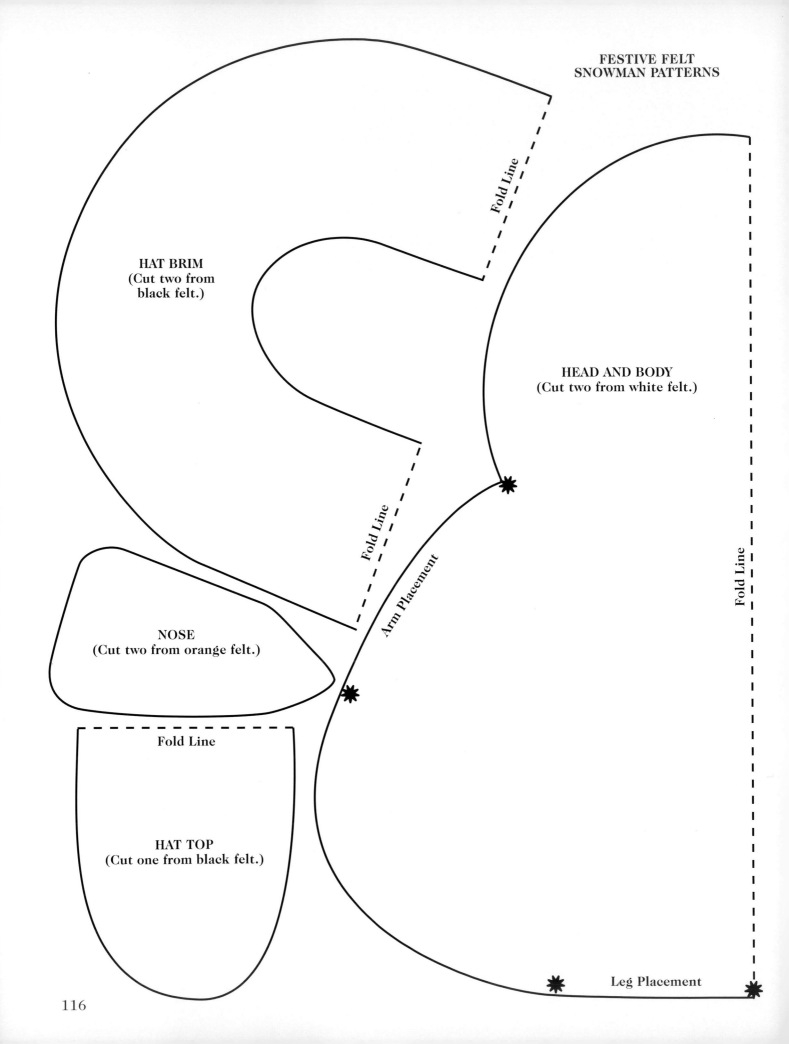

FESTIVE FELT
SNOWMAN PATTERNS

HAT BRIM
(Cut two from
black felt.)

Fold Line

Fold Line

HEAD AND BODY
(Cut two from white felt.)

Fold Line

Arm Placement

NOSE
(Cut two from orange felt.)

Fold Line

HAT TOP
(Cut one from black felt.)

Leg Placement

116

4. To assemble feet and legs, place two foot and leg pieces with right sides together, aligning raw edges. Sew together, leaving short, straight edge unstitched. Trim edges close to seam. Turn right-side out. Stuff firmly with polyester filling to within ⅜" of opening. Baste opening closed, having seams meet at center and toes pointing forward. Repeat with remaining foot and leg pieces. Set aside.

5. On right side of one body piece place short, straight edge of arm along straight edge of body, between dots, as indicated on pattern, making sure thumb is pointing upward. Sew arm to side of body through all thicknesses. Repeat with remaining arm on opposite side of body. Place basted edge of each leg between the *s, as shown on pattern, aligning raw edges and making sure right side of body and fronts of legs are together. Sew legs and body together through all thicknesses.

Note: Toes should face forward when legs are hanging down after stitching.

6. With right sides together, raw edges even, and arms in between body front and body back pieces, baste, then sew body front to body back, leaving bottom open at legs for turning. Clip curves. Turn right-side out. Stuff firmly with polyester filling. Turn raw edges at bottom under ¼" and whipstitch opening closed. Set aside.

7. Cut two nose pieces from orange felt. With right sides together and raw edges even, sew nose pieces together, leaving short, straight edge unstitched. Trim edges close to seam. Turn right-side out. Stuff firmly with polyester filling to within ¼" of opening. Sew gathering stitches around opening. Pull threads tightly to gather end of nose and tie off threads to secure.

8. To mark placement of nose, measure from one side seam to the other side seam at widest part at front of head. Divide measurement in half to find horizontal center of head. Mark horizontal center with straight pin. From horizontal center, run measuring

tape straight up to seam at top center of head. From top center of head, measure down 3" to determine nose placement. Mark. Remove pin. Sew nose in place, sewing gathered end of nose to snowman's head.

9. To mark placement of eyes, measure down 2¾" from top center of head at seam line. Mark with straight pin. Measure ⅝" on each side of pin and mark. Remove pin. Sew one ½" black, ball-type button at each mark.

10. To mark placement of mouth, measure down ¾" from center of nose. Mark. Sew one ¼" black, ball-type button at this point. On each side of this button, measure out ½" from button's center and up ⅛" and mark. Sew remaining ¼" black, ball-type buttons at marks.

11. To mark button placement on body front, measure up 3½" from bottom seam, at center of body, and mark. Sew one 1⅛" flat, black button at this point. From same center point at bottom seam, measure up 2⅛" and mark. Sew remaining 1⅛" flat, black button at this point.

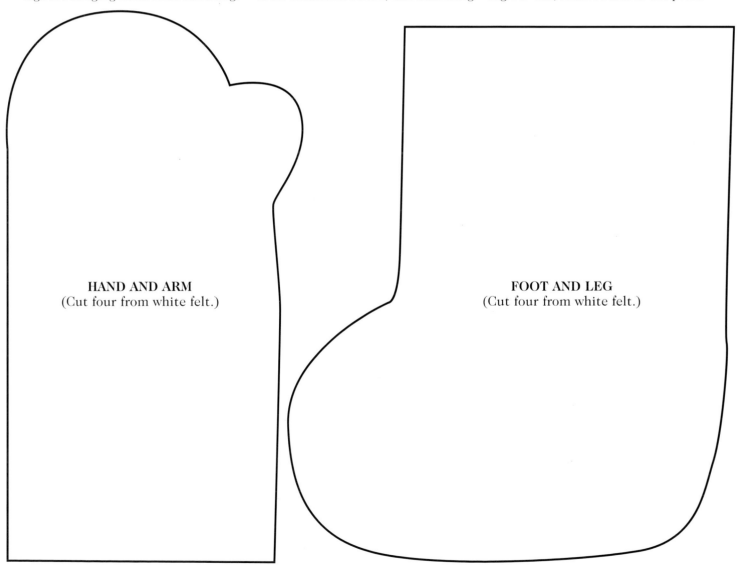

HAND AND ARM
(Cut four from white felt.)

FOOT AND LEG
(Cut four from white felt.)

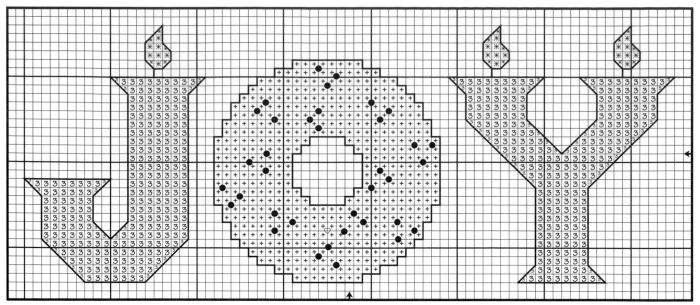

CHRISTMAS HAND TOWELS—JOY

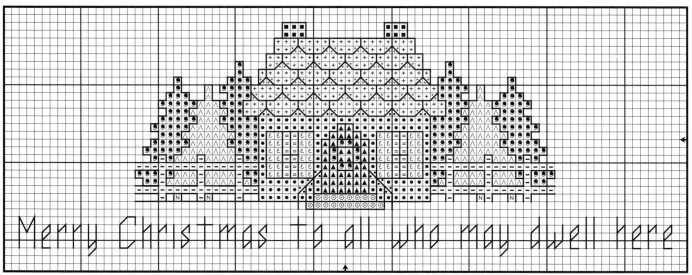

CHRISTMAS HAND TOWELS—MERRY CHRISTMAS

12. Make blush on cheeks by applying tiny amounts of primrose paint to each side of face, using a dry brush and blending paint carefully onto felt.

13. To make hat, cut two brim pieces, one hat top, and one 2½" x 10½" strip for hat sides from black felt. Sew short ends of 2½" x 10½" strip together, placing right sides together, aligning raw edges, and forming a continuous loop. Trim edges close to seam. Turn right-side out. Sew one edge of loop to top of hat, placing right sides together, aligning raw edges, and making sure seam on loop is centered at one long side of hat top. Turn right-side out. Sew the two brim pieces together around outer edges, placing right sides together and aligning raw edges. Trim edges close to seam. Turn right-side out. Baste the two layers of

inner edges of brim together. Sew inner edges of brim to remaining raw edge of loop, placing right sides together and aligning raw edges. Place hat on snowman's head.

14. To make scarf, cut two 1¾" x 20" strips from plaid fabric. Sew the two plaid strips together, placing right sides of fabric together, aligning raw edges, and leaving an opening at one short end for turning. Clip corners. Turn right-side out. Whipstitch opening closed. Press. Tie scarf around snowman's neck.

Christmas Hand Towels

Joy
DMC Color
3 321 red

+ 367 pistachio, dk.
✳ 725 topaz
bs 844 beaver gray, ul. dk.

Fabric: 14-count ecru Park Avenue Fingertips™ towel from Charles Craft, Inc.
Stitch count: 30H x 75W
Design size:

	14-count	2⅛" x 5⅜"
	16-count	1⅞" x 4⅝"
	27-count	2¼" x 5½"
	30-count	2" x 5"

Instructions: Cross stitch using two strands of floss. Backstitch (bs) using one strand 844. Make French knots where • appears at intersecting grid lines, using three strands 321 and wrapping floss around needle twice. Attach ⅜"-wide ribbon bow where ♡ appears on *O*.

118

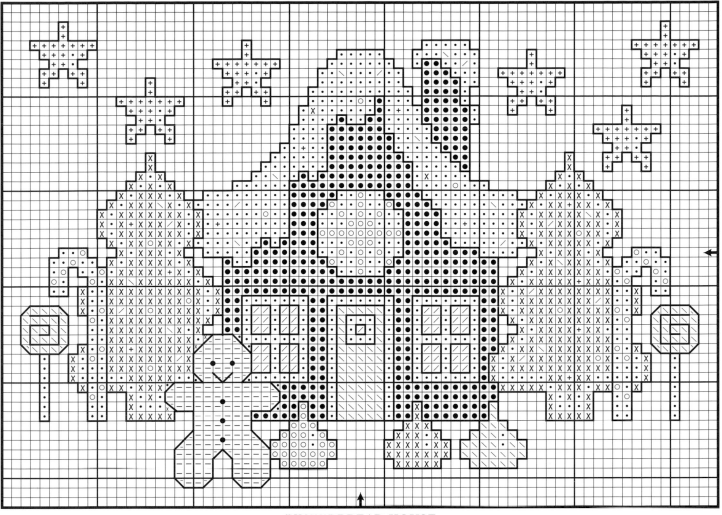

GINGERBREAD HOUSE

Merry Christmas
DMC Color

- • 986 forest, vy. dk.
- ∧ 987 forest, dk.
- − ecru ecru
- + 3328 salmon, med.
- ■ 347 salmon, dk.
- ε 931 antique blue, med.
- = 745 yellow, lt. pl.
- ▲ 436 tan
- ⊙ 648 beaver gray, lt.
- • 3752 antique blue, vy. lt.
- N 435 brown, vy. lt.
- bs 304 red, med.
- bs 844 beaver gray, ul. dk.

Fabric: 14-count ecru with federal green trim Borderlines Fingertips towel from Charles Craft, Inc.

Stitch count: 30H x 84W

Design size:

14-count	2⅛" x 6"
16-count	1⅞" x 5¼"
27-count	2¼" x 6¼"
30-count	2" x 5⅝"

Instructions: Cross stitch using two strands of floss. Backstitch (bs) using one strand of floss.

Backstitch (bs) instructions:

304	lettering
844	remainder of backstitching

Gingerbread House

Anchor®	DMC	Color
• 01	white	white
\ 40	956	geranium
o 46	666	red, bt.
/ 129	800	delft, pl.
X 226	703	chartreuse
+ 291	444	lemon, dk.
• 351	400	mahogany, dk.
− 369	435	brown, vy. lt.
bs 403	310	black

Fabric: 14-count Fiddler's Cloth from Charles Craft, Inc.

Stitch count: 49H x 71W

Design size:

14-count	3½" x 5"
16-count	3" x 4½"
18-count	2¾" x 4"
22-count	2¼" x 3¼"

Instructions: Cross stitch using two strands of floss. Backstitch (bs) using one strand 403/310. Make French knots where symbol • appears at intersecting grid lines, using one strand 403/310 and wrapping floss around needle twice.

FRENCH-KNOT ILLUSTRATION

Doily Pillows

Materials:
Purchased doilies of your choice
Matching **or** complementary fabric
(for backing)
Thread to match fabric
Polyester filling
Disappearing-ink fabric-marking pen

Hand-sewing needle
Scissors
Straight pins
Sewing machine
Iron
2 yds. ⅛"-wide white satin ribbon for **each** pillow (optional)

Note: Doilies with fabric centers and decorative trim will work well for this project.

1. Find right side of doily. Fold trim back toward center of doily, with right sides of trim and doily together. (**Note:** Use the line where trim is attached around perimeter of center of doily as a guide for folding trim back.) Pin.
2. Baste trim to fabric center of doily, ¼" in from folded edge. Remove pins.
3. Cut backing to fit pillow front, leaving a ½" seam allowance.
4. Center backing atop pillow front, placing right sides of fabric together. Pin.
5. Sew around pillow, following previous basting line and leaving an opening for turning. Trim seams, turn, and press.
6. Stuff pillow to desired fullness with polyester filling and whipstitch opening closed.
7. Tack on ribbon bows, if desired.

House Buttons

DMC Color

◤	890	pistachio, ul. dk.
#	909	emerald, vy. dk.
◑	801	coffee, dk.
○	white	white
B	783	gold
ℓ	817	coral red, vy. dk.
Z	3777	terra cotta, vy. dk.
6	648	beaver gray, lt.
✕	932	antique blue, lt.
W	[783	gold
	[817	coral red, vy. dk.
bs	310	black

Fabric: 18-count beige Aida from Zweigart®

Stitch count:
House 1	18H x 23W
House 2	18H x 22W
House 3	19H x 23W

Design size:
14-count	1⅜" x 1⅝"
16-count	1⅛" x 1½"
18-count	1" x 1¼"
22-count	⅞" x 1"

Instructions: Cross stitch using two strands of floss. Backstitch using one

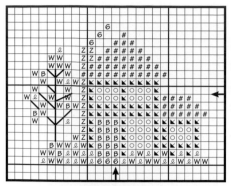

HOUSE 1

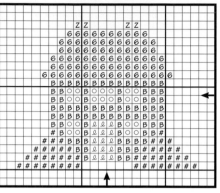

HOUSE 2

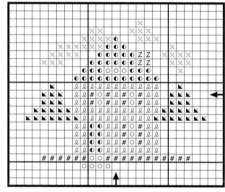

HOUSE 3

strand 310. Cover purchased button forms following manufacturer's instructions.

Note: Buttons must fit through buttonholes on sweater. If buttons do not fit, purchase a conversion kit to transform covered buttons into button covers, and follow manufacturer's instructions to assemble.

Mail Holder

Materials:
11" x 7" piece ¼"-thick Birch plywood
1½"-tall wooden cutout letters (available at craft stores)
Ceramcoat® paints by Delta, colors: Tompte Red, Christmas Green, White
Ceramcoat® Water Base Satin Varnish

Founder's Adhesive™ **or** other tacky glue
Paintbrushes, sizes: #0, #6
1"-wide sponge brush
½"-long nails
Fine sandpaper
Toothpicks
Stylus
Hammer
Scroll saw

1. Cut two 3" x 7" pieces and one 5" x 7" piece of plywood. Sand all pieces. Nail plywood pieces together, using one 3" x 7" piece for bottom of mail holder, one 3" x 7" piece for front, and one 5" x 7" piece for back. Refer to photo on page **109** for arrangement of wood pieces.
2. Paint top edges of mail holder white, and remainder of holder red, using sponge brush. Let dry.
3. Paint cutout letters white, using #6 paintbrush. Let dry. Freehand paint Christmas Green holly leaves on letters, using #0 paintbrush. Let dry. Add red holly berries, and red dot around perimeter of each letter, using stylus. Let dry.
4. Apply thin coat of glue to back side of letters, using toothpick. Press letters to front of mail holder.
5. Apply two coats of varnish to mail holder, allowing piece to dry thoroughly between coats and after second coat.

Painted Photo Frames

Note: For these projects, a general materials list has been given. Specific materials for each project have been listed separately.

General materials:
Two 4" x 6" acrylic photo frames
Two 4" x 6" pieces white paper (optional)
Pencil

Teacher's Photo Frame
Materials:
Duncan's 3-Dimensional Scribbles® Fabric Writers paints, colors: SC 112 Bright Yellow, SC 121 Bright Red, SC 126 Bright Blue, SC 133 Christmas Green, SC 110 White, SC 139 Black

Christmas Bulbs Frame
Materials:
Duncan's 3-Dimensional Scribbles® Fabric Writers paints, colors: SC 110 White, SC 121 Bright Red, SC 134 Bright Green, SC 139 Black, SC 301 Crystal, SC 203 Glittering Gold

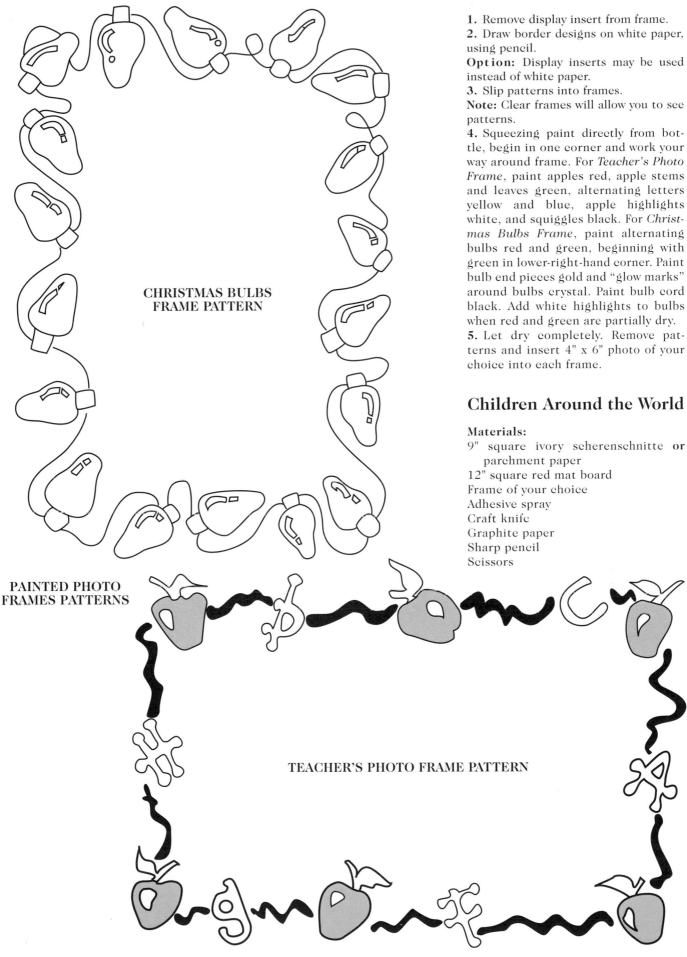

CHRISTMAS BULBS FRAME PATTERN

PAINTED PHOTO FRAMES PATTERNS

TEACHER'S PHOTO FRAME PATTERN

1. Remove display insert from frame.
2. Draw border designs on white paper, using pencil.

Option: Display inserts may be used instead of white paper.

3. Slip patterns into frames.

Note: Clear frames will allow you to see patterns.

4. Squeezing paint directly from bottle, begin in one corner and work your way around frame. For *Teacher's Photo Frame*, paint apples red, apple stems and leaves green, alternating letters yellow and blue, apple highlights white, and squiggles black. For *Christmas Bulbs Frame*, paint alternating bulbs red and green, beginning with green in lower-right-hand corner. Paint bulb end pieces gold and "glow marks" around bulbs crystal. Paint bulb cord black. Add white highlights to bulbs when red and green are partially dry.

5. Let dry completely. Remove patterns and insert 4" x 6" photo of your choice into each frame.

Children Around the World

Materials:
9" square ivory scherenschnitte **or** parchment paper
12" square red mat board
Frame of your choice
Adhesive spray
Craft knife
Graphite paper
Sharp pencil
Scissors

1. Cut out pattern.
2. Fold paper in half crosswise and then lengthwise. Place pattern atop folded paper, aligning broken lines on pattern with folds. Transfer pattern, using graphite paper and pencil.
3. Use craft knife to cut along pattern lines through all layers of paper. Carefully unfold paper.
4. Spray back side of paper cutting with an even coat of adhesive and press cutting to center of mat board. Frame as desired.

Papier Tole Snowman

Materials:

Package of four pre-cut snowman silhouettes on antique parchment paper (**Note:** Designer used Wee Christmas Snowman Silhouettes, No. 312 from Tree Toys.)
Acrylic paints, colors: Christmas red, Christmas green, white, yellow, black, brown
4"-diameter natural twig wreath
Small amount clear glitter
DecoArt™ Snow-Tex™ Textural Medium
12" length 2½"-wide red velvet craft ribbon
10" length metallic-gold braid (for hanger)
1½ yds. 1½"-wide red, green, and metallic-gold plaid ribbon (for bow)
10" wooden kitchen skewer **or** ⅛"-diameter wood dowel
Two 2" silk evergreen sprigs
Three ¼"-diameter red plastic berries
4" length fine-gauge floral wire
Glass Kote clear lacquer and thinner
Creatively Yours® clear silicone glue
Paintbrushes: fine liner and ½"
Craft stick (for spreading Snow-Tex™)
Low-temperature glue gun and glue sticks
Pencil with eraser
Small, sharp scissors
Ruler
Wire cutters
Tweezers
Toothpicks
Waxed paper

Finished size: 5" x 12"

Note: Please read all instructions carefully before beginning. The dimensional effect of papier tole is achieved by cutting, shaping, and layering several identical paper figures such as these snowman silhouettes. Art prints and greeting cards can also be used. Tiny raised mounds of clear silicone

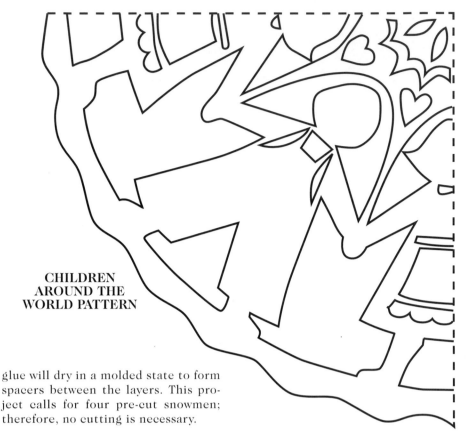

CHILDREN AROUND THE WORLD PATTERN

glue will dry in a molded state to form spacers between the layers. This project calls for four pre-cut snowmen; therefore, no cutting is necessary.

1. Before painting the four snowmen, lightly pencil in lines to separate hat and mittens from snowman's body. Also use pencil to extend hat brim over broom and outline mitten holding candy cane. Edge with pencil short pipe stem and broom handle, as well.
2. Cover working surface with waxed paper. Paint three snowmen identically on **one side only** as follows, using liner brush. Paint bodies white, hats black, brooms and pipe yellow, broom handles and pipe stems brown, mittens green, and candy cane red-and-white striped. On remaining snowman, paint hat, mittens, and candy cane to match first three figures. Leave remainder of this snowman unpainted. Let snowmen dry.
3. To shape first three fully painted snowmen, one at a time, keep each intact and turn painted-side down in palm of your hand. Gently press edges repeatedly with round end of pencil eraser to "cup" up. When figures are placed painted-sides up, snowmen should cup under. When shaping, be careful not to wrinkle paper excessively or to crack paint. Save partially painted fourth snowman for later use.
Note: Before you shape painted snowmen as described in this step, use procedure described to practice "cupping" a small, circular scrap of paper first.
4. To give depth to figure, glue snowmen together in three stacked layers.

Place first snowman right-side up atop work surface. Squeeze from tube approximately six tiny, raised mounds of silicone glue as follows: one on hat, another on broom, one on mitten holding candy cane, and three evenly spaced on body. Leave glue in mounds and break off from tube each time, using toothpick. Place second snowman atop first, using clean toothpick to align one snowman with the other. (**Note:** Do not flatten glue.) View figure from all angles and push visible glue from edges, using toothpick. Wait ten minutes for glue to dry and repeat process by gluing third snowman atop second. While second layer of glue dries, cut off painted portions of fourth snowman. This includes: hat, right mitten, and left mitten with candy cane attached. Gently cup pieces separately in palm of your hand as described in Step 3. When last layer of glue has dried, place a tiny, raised mound of glue on back of each shaped cutout. Align cutouts atop snowman, using tweezers and toothpick. Remove any visible glue from edges, using toothpick. While glue dries, frost twig wreath with Snow-Tex™, referring to photo on page **113** and using craft stick.
5. To finish snowman, paint black dots for eye and three buttons, using tip of toothpick. When paint dots are dry, spread a thick, flat coat of silicone on **white body only**, using toothpick. Sprinkle with clear

glitter snow and shake off excess. Brush on two heavy coats of lacquer to remaining painted areas, using ½" paintbrush and waiting one hour between coats.

6. To make red ribbon backing, "V" cut bottom end by gently folding ribbon in half vertically and cutting ribbon at an angle from outside edge up 1½" toward fold. To shape top, fold corners at opposite end of ribbon to center back to make an inverted "V." Glue folds in place, using low-temperature glue gun. Glue skewer or dowel vertically to center back of ribbon for support and glue ends of metallic braid on each side of dowel to form hanging loop, using low-temperature glue gun.

7. Make a multi-loop bow measuring 5" across with three loops on each side and 3"–4" streamers. Secure bow center with floral wire, twisting on back. Glue to top of inverted "V," using low-temperature glue gun.

8. To finish, glue wreath to ribbon approximately 3" from bottom, using low-temperature glue gun. Glue snowman to ribbon in center of wreath, two 2" evergreen sprigs on front of wreath at bottom, and three berries clustered in center of sprigs, using low-temperature glue gun. Trim greens shorter, if needed, using wire cutters.

Apple and Cinnamon Tree

Materials:
4–6 red-skinned apples
8-oz. bottle concentrated lemon juice
12" square white poster board
12" square red foil
Fifteen 10mm jingle bells
16mm jingle bell
Five 3"-long cinnamon sticks
30" length 1"-wide ivory cotton trim
Press-on cloth picture hanger
Knife **or** electric food slicer
4 yds. ⅛"-wide red ribbon
Tacky glue
Spray glue
White craft glue
Scissors
Craft knife
Newspaper

1. Cut apples into ⅛"-thick slices, cutting across center of apples to attain star design in center of each slice. Apples may be cut by hand or with an electric food slicer for thin, even slices.

2. Soak apple slices in lemon juice for five minutes. Drain and place on newspaper to dry.

3. Trace tree pattern on white poster board. Lay poster board flat atop hard surface and cut around tree pattern, using sharp craft knife.

4. Lay tree pattern atop wrong side of red foil. Trace pattern on foil, adding ¼" to outside diameter. Cut out foil. Lay foil right-side down atop newspaper. Spray wrong side of foil evenly with spray glue. Position poster-board tree onto wrong side of red foil. Press board to foil. Bring extra foil up and over edges of poster-board tree, mitering at corners.

5. On back side of tree, lay bead of white glue along edge of tree body. Do not glue around tree trunk. Press nondecorative edge of eyelet atop glue, placing so that decorative edge extends out from tree, forming a frame around tree.

6. Choose fifteen uniform apple slices to arrange on tree. Carefully pick up one slice at a time, apply tacky glue to back of slice, and press in place on tree, referring to photo on page **113** for placement.

7. Glue five cinnamon sticks to trunk of tree, placing horizontally.

8. Glue one small bell to center of **each** apple slice and one large bell at top of cinnamon trunk.

9. Cut fifteen 4" lengths from ribbon. Thread ribbon through top of **each** bell and tie into a bow. Trim ribbon ends. Thread two 12" pieces of ribbon through large bell and tie into a bow. Trim ribbon ends.

10. Center and press cloth picture hanger toward top of back side of tree.

½ of pattern is shown.

APPLE AND CINNAMON TREE PATTERN

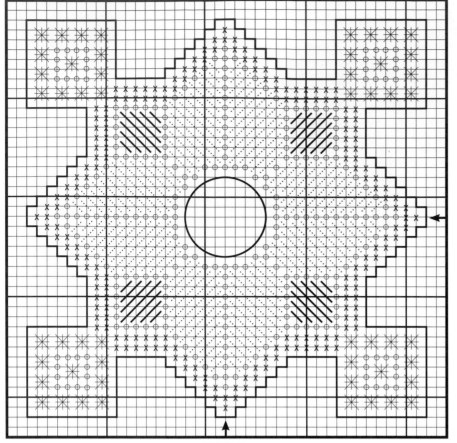

TAG 1

Ribbon and Bead Package Tags

Tag 1

Kreinik

1/16"

	Ribbon	Color	Stitch
X	003HL	red	Cross stitch
✳	003HL	red	Smyrna cross
╱	009HL	emerald	Slanting Gobelin
⟋	015HL	chartreuse	Slanting Gobelin

Mill Hill Glass Seed Beads

○ 2011   Victorian gold
(Note: Two packages will make all three tags.)

Tag 2

Kreinik

1/16"

	Ribbon	Color	Stitch
X	009HL	emerald	Cross stitch
✳	003HL	red	Smyrna cross
╱	009HL	emerald	Slanting Gobelin
⟋	015HL	chartreuse	Slanting Gobelin

Mill Hill Glass Seed Beads

○ 2011   Victorian gold
(Note: Two packages will make all three tags.)

Tag 3

Kreinik

1/16"

	Ribbon	Color	Stitch
X	009HL	emerald	Cross stitch
△	003HL	red	Cross stitch
✳	009HL	emerald	Smyrna cross
W	003HL	red	Smyrna cross
╱	003HL	red	Slanting Gobelin
⟋	015HL	chartreuse	Slanting Gobelin

Mill Hill Glass Seed Beads

○ 2011   Victorian gold
(Note: Two packages will make all three tags.)

Fabric: 14-mesh ivory plastic canvas
Stitch count: 40H x 40W
Design size:

11-count	3⅝" x 3⅝"
14-count	2⅞" x 2⅞"
16-count	2½" x 2½"
18-count	2¼" x 2¼"

Instructions: Work beaded portion of design first, attaching beads with half-cross stitches and using quilting thread and #10 crewel needle. Work remainder of design according to chart, using 18" lengths of Kreinik 1/16" metallic ribbon and #24 tapestry needle.

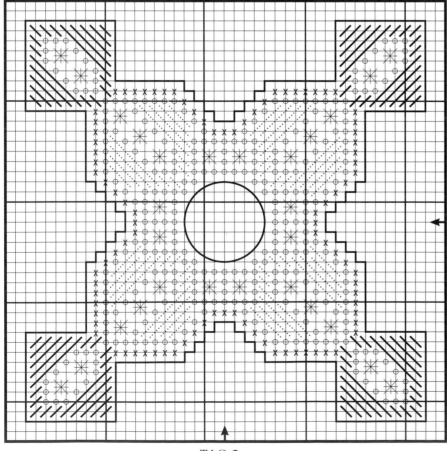

TAG 2

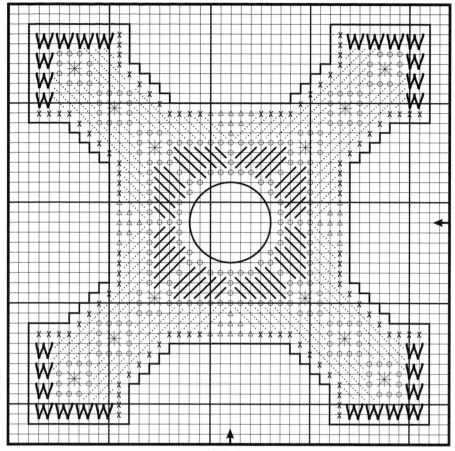

TAG 3

Note: Materials listed will make one set of three, one-sided package tags. Designs can also be used as tree ornaments. To make reversible ornaments, purchase additional materials, stitch two identical pieces for **each** ornament, and whipstitch pieces together around perimeter.

1. Complete stitching following instructions given.

2. Place completed stitched piece atop cutting surface. Carefully trim away excess canvas, using plastic-canvas cutter and following outline of stitched design.

Note: Refer to heavy, dark outline on chart.

3. To mount cabochon in center of stitched design, apply a small amount of glue to back of cabochon, using toothpick, and press cabochon in place for 30 seconds. Let glue dry thoroughly before proceeding.

Note: If not using cabochons, fill in center circle with an equivalent color of seed beads.

4. To make backing, place cut-out design atop unstitched canvas square and cut latter to same size and shape as stitched square.

5. To finish, place front and backing pieces together, aligning edges and holes. Whipstitch together along edges, using metallic-gold ribbon and crewel needle.

Option: To use as an ornament, glue a metallic-gold ribbon hanging loop to back side near top.

Helpful hints for stitching: To work with seed beads, thread #10 crewel needle with quilting thread and draw needle up through canvas hole at lower left of first stitch, leaving a tail to catch under first several stitches. Attach beads individually with half-cross stitches, working from lower-left to upper-right corner of each stitch and referring to chart. Work horizontal rows from left to right **or** from right to left, making sure all half-cross stitches slant in the same direction. Work vertical and diagonal rows from top to bottom. When moving from one area to another or when beginning and ending a thread, anchor thread by weaving it through stitching on back. If any beads appear loose, stitch through them a second time. To straighten a long row of beads, run needle back through entire row. To work remainder of design, thread #24 tapestry needle with 18" length metallic ribbon, cut on the diagonal to prevent raveling. Work cross stitches, Smyrna crosses, and slanting Gobelin stitches, referring to chart. For best results, keep ribbon smooth and flat. To prevent twisting and tangling, guide ribbon between thumb and forefinger of free hand while completing each stitch. Drop needle occasionally to allow ribbon to unwind. Check your work from the back. Weave ends of ribbon securely through stitching on back and clip ribbon ends.

Materials:

Three 40-hole squares 14-mesh ivory plastic canvas (for backing)
One 10mm reel Kreinik Balger® metallic 1/16" ribbon, color: Gold (002HL)
#24 tapestry needle
#10 crewel needle
Quilting thread
Plastic-canvas cutter
One **each** 18mm round acrylic cabochons, colors: Topaz, Ruby, Emerald (or colors of your choice) (**Note:** Designer used acrylic cabochons from The Beadery.)
Goop Glue (from American Art Clay Co.)
Scissors
Toothpicks

Finished size: 4" x 4" (diagonal measure)

SLANTING GOBELIN STITCH

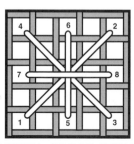

SMYRNA CROSS STITCH

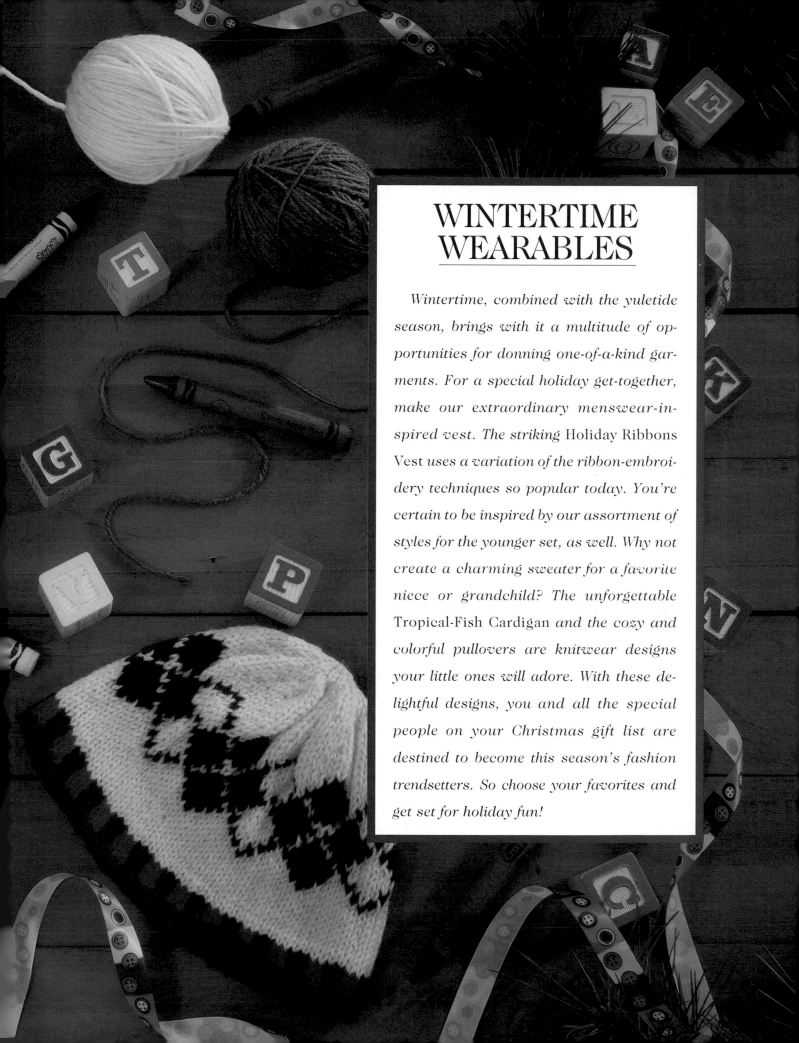

WINTERTIME WEARABLES

Wintertime, combined with the yuletide season, brings with it a multitude of opportunities for donning one-of-a-kind garments. For a special holiday get-together, make our extraordinary menswear-inspired vest. The striking Holiday Ribbons Vest uses a variation of the ribbon-embroidery techniques so popular today. You're certain to be inspired by our assortment of styles for the younger set, as well. Why not create a charming sweater for a favorite niece or grandchild? The unforgettable Tropical-Fish Cardigan and the cozy and colorful pullovers are knitwear designs your little ones will adore. With these delightful designs, you and all the special people on your Christmas gift list are destined to become this season's fashion trendsetters. So choose your favorites and get set for holiday fun!

Festive Fashions

When it comes to wearable fashions, the holidays provide fabulous inspiration for creating. It is an opportunity to break out and enjoy seasonal clothing that is certain to be admired by all who see it. Whether you choose to make sweaters for your favorite little ones, craft a trendy vest for a special friend, or don your own handiwork for a festive gathering, you're certain to enjoy the compliments you receive.

Right—*Easy-to-make satin-ribbon embellishments, plus embroidery and a scattering of beads, transform a plain black vest into our* **Holiday Ribbons Vest.** *This is an ideal garment for a dressy Christmas party. Pair the vest with a velvet skirt and a pretty blouse to create a dazzling look for a special evening! Instructions begin on page 137.*

Above—*This fashionable, menswear-inspired vest will stand out at holiday parties! The* **Crazy-Quilt Vest** *uses fusible web for easy construction, and provides a great use for your scraps of dark, menswear fabrics. Decorative trims add a festive touch to the vest, and three frog closures give it extra pizzazz. You can create this wardrobe addition by using any vest pattern, which makes this a convenient project—you probably already have all the necessary materials in your scrap bag and notions drawer. Instructions are on page 137.*

Left and opposite—*Your little one will be a fashion trendsetter when she dons this colorful sweater you have knit using simple stockinette stitch. She and her friends will love the vivid colors and the underwater scene where bright pink fish "swim" past embroidered green seaweed. The blue-green background color flecked with white creates an "ocean" home for the tropical designs that decorate the sweater's front and back. She is sure to be a scene-stealer wherever she wears this charming* **Tropical-Fish Cardigan.** *Why not wrap this beauty in patterned or colored tissue paper and place it under the tree as a special gift from Mom on Christmas Day? Instructions begin on page 135.*

Left—*Bright yellow yarn, combined with red and navy, was used to create this adorable* **Child's Argyle Pullover and Hat.** *Knit with basic stockinette stitch, this two-piece ensemble will keep your youngster warm in eye-catching style all through the cold-weather season. Instructions begin on page 134.*

Opposite—*Designed to stand up to the rough-and-tumble life-style of children, this easy-care sweater, with its simple pattern stitch, will be easy to knit. This* **Six-Color Pullover** *looks super with blue jeans and, in this day of unisex dressing, is appropriate for both boys and girls. Let this sweater accompany your child back to school after the holidays and throughout the remainder of winter. Instructions are on page 134.*

Six-Color Pullover

Materials:
Plymouth Emu Superwash Double Knit 50-gram (1.75 oz./123-yds.) skeins, colors: black #3070 [5 (6, 7, 8, 9) skeins], yellow #3095 (1 skein), blue #3013 (one skein), red #3051 (one skein), green #3087 (one skein), purple #3052 (one skein)
Straight knitting needles, sizes 8 and 10 **or** sizes needed to obtain gauge
Yarn needle

Gauge: In pat, st with two strands yarn and larger needles, 24 sts and 40 rows = 6".
Make gauge swatch as follows: With larger needles and two strands black yarn, CO 24 sts. Work pat st for 40 rows. Swatch should measure 6" square. If it does not, p one row on right side of fabric to mark difference. If swatch is too narrow, change to larger needles. If swatch is too wide, change to smaller needles. Work even for 6" to prove gauge.

Size: 4 (6, 8, 10, 12)
Body chest size: 23" (25", 27", 28½", 30")
Finished chest size: 25½" (27", 30", 31½", 33")
Finished length: 15" (16", 17", 18½", 20¼")

Construction note: This sweater is made with two strands of yarn and in four pieces: one back, one front, and two sleeves. After pieces are completed, the right shoulder seam is joined. Sts are then picked up around neck and a k 1, p 1 ribbed band is added. Work with two strands yarn held together throughout. Carry black yarn along edge of work. Join contrasting colors at beg of Row 3; after Row 4 cut contrasting color strand, leaving 3" to weave in later.

Pat st: (multiple of 3 sts + 3; a rep of 20 rows)
Row 1 (right side): K with black.
Row 2: P with black.
Row 3: With red, k 1, *wyib sl 1, k 2; rep from * ending wyib sl 1, k 1.
Row 4: With red, k 1, * wyif sl 1, wyib k 2; rep from * ending wyif sl 1, wyib k 1.
Rows 5, 9, 13, & 17: Rep Row 1.
Rows 6, 10, 14, & 18: Rep Row 2.
Row 7: With yellow, rep Row 3.
Row 8: With yellow, rep Row 4.
Row 11: With green, rep Row 3.
Row 12: With green, rep Row 4.
Row 15: With blue, rep Row 3.
Row 16: With blue, rep Row 4.
Row 19: With purple, rep Row 3.
Row 20: With purple, rep Row 4.

Pullover
Back: Beg at bottom edge with smaller needles and 2 strands black, CO 50 (54, 60, 62, 66) sts. Work k 1, p 1 ribbing for 1½" (1½", 1½", 2", 2"), inc 1 (0, 0, 1, 0) st on last row. Change to larger needles and beg pat st. Work even for 4". Check gauge; piece should measure 12¾" (13½", 15", 15¾", 16½") wide. Work even to about 10" (10½", 11", 12" 13") from beg, ending ready to work a black knit row.
Back armhole shaping: At beg of nxt 2 rows, BO 6 sts—39 (42, 48, 51, 54) sts. Cont est pat to 15" (16", 17", 18½", 20") from beg, ending ready to work a black knit row. With black, BO straight across.
Front: Work as for Back to 11½" (12½", 13½", 15", 16½") from beg, ending ready to work a black knit row.
Neck shaping: Work 17 (18, 20, 21, 22) sts; attach new strands and BO center 5 (6, 8, 9, 10) sts; work to end of row. Working each side with separate strands, BO at each neck edge every other row 2 sts twice and 1 st 3 times. When piece is same length as Back, ending ready to work a black knit row, with black BO rem 10 (11, 13, 14, 15) sts for each shoulder.
Sleeves (make two): With smaller needles and 2 strands black, CO 24 (26, 28, 30, 30) sts. Work 1½" k 1, p 1 ribbing, inc 0 (1, 2, 3, 3) sts evenly spaced across last row—24 (27, 30, 33, 33) sts. Change to larger needles and pat st. Cont in est pat, inc 1 st each edge (including new sts into pat) every 8th row 7 (7, 7, 7, 8) times—38 (41, 44, 47, 49) sts. When piece is 11 (11¾", 11¾", 12¼", 13") from beg, ending ready to work a black knit row, BO with black.

Finishing: Join right shoulder seam.
Neck band: With rs facing and using smaller needles and 2 strands black, pick up and k 54 (56, 60, 62, 64) sts around neck leaving 10 (11, 13, 14, 15) shoulder sts on back. Work ¾" k 1, p 1 ribbing. BO in ribbing. Join left shoulder and neck-band seam. Sew sleeve and side seams. Set in sleeves. Weave in loose ends.

Child's Argyle Pullover and Hat

Materials:
Coats & Clark Red Heart Super Sport Yarn Art. E. 271 (3 oz./279-yds.) skeins, colors: yellow #230 [2 (2, 2, 3) skeins], navy #861 (1 skein), jockey red #904 (1 skein)
Straight knitting needles, sizes 5 and 7 **or** sizes needed to obtain gauge
Four ⅜" buttons of your choice
Yarn needle

Gauge: In St st with larger needles, 20 sts and 24 rows = 4".
Make gauge swatch as follows: With larger needles and yellow, CO 20 sts. Work St st for 24 rows. Swatch should measure 4" square. If it does not, p one row on right side of fabric to mark difference. If swatch is too narrow, change to larger needles. If swatch is too wide, change to smaller needles. Work even for 4" to prove gauge.

Size: 12 mo. (2T, 3T, 4T)
Body chest size: 20" (21", 22", 23")
Finished chest size: 21½" (23", 25", 27")

Finished length: 13½" (14", 15", 16")

Construction note: This sweater is made in four pieces: one back, one front, and two sleeves. After pieces are completed and joined, sts are picked up around front and back necks and two-color border is added.

Pat st: (multiple of 4 sts; a rep of 4 rows).
Row 1 (rs): With red, k 1, * sl 2 wyib, k 2; rep from *, ending sl 2, k 1.
Row 2: With red, k 1, * sl 2 wyif, p 2; rep from *, ending sl 2, k 1.
Row 3: With navy, k 1, * k 2, sl 2 wyib; rep from *, ending k 3.
Row 4: With navy, k 1, * p 2, sl 2 wyif; rep from *, ending p 2, k1.

Notes: When instructed to sl 2, slip 2 sts purlwise on every row. On all rs rows, sl sts wyib, and on all ws rows, sl sts wyif. The argyle pat is worked from the chart. Read chart from right to left for rs rows and from left to right for ws rows. Carry color not in use loosely across ws of work; twist strands at color changes.

Pullover

Back: Beg at bottom edge with smaller needles and navy, CO 52 (56, 60, 68) sts. P 1 row.
Striped border: Rep pat st rows 1–4 twice. Break off red and navy, leaving 6" strands to weave in later. Change to larger needles and k 1 row, inc 4 (4, 2, 2) sts evenly spaced—56 (60, 62, 70) sts. Work 7 more rows St st. Keeping 1 st each edge in yellow, work chart, beg with Row 1 at #1 and working to #16, 3 (3, 3, 4) times; then work #1–#6 (#1–#10, #1–#12, #1–#4) once.
Row 2: Work #6–#1 (#10–#1, #12–#1, #4–#1); then rep from #16–#1, 3 (3, 3, 4) times. Work est chart pat to completion. Break off navy. With yellow, work St st beg with a p row for 4". Check gauge; not including edge sts,

piece should measure 10¾" (11½", 12½", 13½") wide. Work even to 13" (13½" 14½", 15½") from beg, ending with a ws row.
Back neck shaping: K 14 (16, 17, 21) sts; attach a new skein of yellow and BO center 28 sts; work rem sts. Work sides separately and at same time to 13½" (14", 15", 16") from beg. BO shoulder sts.
Front: Work as for Back to 11" (11½", 12½", 13½") from beg, ending with a ws row.
Note: To work chart, keep 1 st each edge in yellow; then beg Row 1 at #7 (#11, #13, #5) and work to #16; rep #1–#16, 2 (3, 3, 3) times; rep from #1–#12 (#1–#4, #1–#8, #1–#8) once.
Row 2: Work from #12–#1 (#4–#1, #8–#1, #8–#1); rep from #16–#1, 2 (3, 3, 3) times and from #16–#7 (#16–#11, #16–#13, #16–#5) once.
Front Neck Shaping: Work 21 (23, 24, 28) sts; attach a new skein of yellow and BO center 16 sts; work rem sts. Working sides separately and at once, BO eor at each neck edge 3 sts once, 2 sts once, and 1 st twice. When piece is same length as Back, BO 14 (16, 17, 21) sts for each shoulder.
Sleeves (make two): Beg at cuff with navy and smaller needles, CO 28 (32, 32, 36) sts. Work pat st rows 1–4, four times. Break off red and navy. Change to larger needles and beg with a k row, work yellow St st, alternating inc 1 st each edge every 2nd row; then every 4th row until 26 total sts have been added—54 (58, 58, 62) sts. When piece is 10" (10", 10½", 11") from beg, BO straight across.
Finishing: Join right shoulder seam.
Front border: With rs facing and using smaller needles and yellow, pick up and k 4 sts around front neck to shoulder. Break off yellow. With navy, p 1 row. Work pat st rows 1–4 twice. Break off red. With navy, k 1 row, then BO knitwise.

Color code:	
■	Navy
□	Yellow

Back border: Work as for Front Border, picking up 36 sts only.
Button band: With rs facing and using smaller needles and navy, pick up and k 8 sts along front border edge. K 1 row. Nxt row, k 2, yo, k 2 tog, k 1, yo, k 2 tog, k 1. K 1 row. BO knitwise. Rep for second neckband edge. Sew buttons to Back Border, opposite buttonholes. Place markers 6" (6½", 6½", 7") each side of shoulder seams. Set in sleeves between markers. Join underarm and side seams. Weave in loose ends.

Hat

Beg at lower edge with larger needles and navy, CO 96 sts. P 1 row. Work pat st rows 1–4 twice. Break off red and navy. With yellow, k 1 row, inc 2 sts. Work 7 more rows St st. Keeping 1 st each edge in yellow, work chart from #1–#16, 6 times. Break off navy after completion of chart. With yellow, work 5 rows St st, beg with a p row.
Crown Shaping, Row 1: K 2, * k 2 tog, k 6; rep from * across.
Row 2: P 86 sts.
Row 3: K 2, * k 2 tog, k 4; rep from * across.
Row 4: P 72 sts.
Row 5: * K 2 tog, k 2; rep from * across.
Row 6: P 54 sts.
Row 7: * K 2 tog across.
Row 8: P 27 sts.
Row 9: K 1, * k 2 tog across.
Row 10: P 14 sts.
Break yarn, leaving 18" strand. With yarn needle, thread strand though rem sts. Pull strand tightly to gather for top of hat. Using same strand, join hat seam to color border; then use navy to join this border. Weave in loose ends.

Tropical-Fish Cardigan

Materials:

King Cole Big Value Double Knit 100-gram (3.5 oz./320 yds., 100% worsted-weight acrylic), skeins, colors: Kingfisher #129 (*A*) (2 skeins), White #001 (*B*) (1 skein), Bright Pink #206 (*C*) (1 skein)

Several yds. **each** double knitting yarn, colors: kelly green, light green (for embroidery)

1 yd. **each** Krinkles™ gathered ribbon, colors: Apple Green #550, Emerald #580

Washable fabric adhesive (**Note:** Designer used Beacon's Fabritac.)

Six 7/16" buttons

Straight knitting needles, sizes 5 and 6 **or** sizes needed to obtain gauge

Five stitch holders

32 31 30 29 28 27 26 25 24 23 22 21 20 19 18 17 16 15 14 13 12 11 10 9 8 7 6 5 4 3 2 #1

CHILD'S ARGYLE PULLOVER AND HAT CHART

Knitting Abbreviations:

beg—begin(ning)
BO—bind off
CO—cast on
dec—decrease(ing)
inc—increase(ing)
m—make a stitch
nxt—next
rem—remaining
rep—repeat
s2sk—sl 2 tog as if to k, sl 1 as if to k, reinsert left-hand needle into 3 s sts and k tog
sl st(s)—slip stitch(es)
ssk—slip slip knit: slip 2 sts knit-wise singly to right-hand needle, insert left-hand needle through the front of the 2 sts, and k 2 tog
st(s)—stitch(es)
St st—Stockinette stitch
ws—wrong side
wyif—with yarn in front
yo—yarn over

Two stitch markers
Tapestry needle

Gauge: In stockinette stitch with larger needles, 5 sts and 8 rows = 1".

Size: 2 (4, 6, 8, 10)
Body chest size: 21" (23", 25", 27", 29")
Finished chest size: 25½" (27½", 29½", 31½", 33½")
Finished length: 16" (17", 18", 19", 20")

Construction note: This sweater is made in three pieces: one body and two sleeves. After pieces are completed and assembled, stitches are picked up for the button band and worked in k1, p1 rib.

Cardigan

Body: With smaller needles and A, CO 111 (121, 131, 141, 151) sts.
Row 1 (right side): K 1, * p 1, k 1; rep from *.
Row 2: P 1, * k 1, p 1. Work in established ribbing for 1½", inc 12 (10, 12, 10, 12) sts evenly in last row—123 (131, 143, 151, 163) sts.
With larger needles and working in St st, begin chart 1. Work as established until 9½" (10", 10½", 11", 11½") from beg, ending with ready to work a ws row. Nxt row, work on 31 (33, 36, 38, 41) sts, place marker, work nxt 61 (65, 71, 75, 81) sts, place marker, work to end of row.
Shape neck: Dec 1 st at each edge of nxt row, then again every 4th row 12 (12, 13, 13, 14) times more while continuing chart as established. AT THE SAME TIME, when piece measures 10½"

(11", 11½", 12", 12½") from beg, ending after a ws row, start armhole shaping.
Right front armhole shaping: Work across to first marker, turn, leaving rem sts on holder. Dec 1 st at armhole edge every other row 4 times. Once neck shaping is complete, work even until 16" (17", 18", 19", 20") from beg, leaving rem 14 (16, 18, 20, 22) sts on holder.
Back: Work across sts between markers, dec at both ends to shape armhole. Work even until same length as for front, then leave rem 53 (57, 63, 67, 73) sts on holder as follows: 14 (16, 18, 20, 22) sts on first holder, 25 (25, 27, 27, 29) sts on 2nd holder, and 14 (16, 18, 20, 22) sts on 3rd holder.
Left front: Work as for right front on rem sts.
Sleeves (make two): With smaller needles and A, CO 33 (33, 35, 35, 37) sts. Work in ribbing as for body for 1½" (1½", 2", 2", 2") inc 6 (6, 8, 8, 10) sts evenly across last row—39 (39, 43, 43, 47) sts. With larger needle and in St st, begin chart 1. At same time, inc 1 st each end every 6th row 0 (8, 6, 13, 10) times, then every 8th row 7 (2, 4, 0, 3) times—53 (59, 63, 69, 73) sts. Work even until 9" (10", 11", 12", 13") from beg.
Shape armhole: Dec 1 st each end every other row 4 times—45 (51, 55, 61, 65) sts. BO all sts.

Fish

Make four. With larger needles and C, CO 5 sts.
Row 1: Sl 2 wyif, p 1, sl 2 wyif.
Row 2: K 2, m 1, k 1, m 1, k 2.
Row 3: Sl 2 wyif, m 1, p 3, m 1, sl 2 wyif.
Row 4: K 2, m 1, k 5, m 1, k 2.
Row 5: Sl 2 wyif, m 1, p 7, m 1, sl 2 wyif.
Row 6: K 2, m 1, k 9, m 1, k 2.
Row 7: Sl 2 wyif, p 11, sl 2 wyif.
Row 8: K 2, k 11, k 2.
Row 9: Sl 2 wyif, k 11, sl 2 wyif.
Row 10: K 2, m 1, k 11, m 1, k 2.
Row 11: Sl 2 wyif, (k 1, p 1) 6 times, k 1, sl 2 wyif.
Row 12: K 2, k 13, k 2.
Row 13: Sl 2 wyif, (p 1, k 1) 6 times, p 1, sl 2 wyif.
Row 14: K 2, m 1, k 13, m 1, k 2.
Row 15: Sl 2 wyif, m 1, (p 1, k 1) 7 times, p 1, m 1, sl 2 wyif.
Row 16: K 2, m 1, k 17, m 1, k 2.
Row 17: P 2 tog, p 1, pull right-most st on right-hand needle over nxt st for first BO. BO 4 more sts. Sl 1 wyif, (k 1, p 1) 6 times, k 1, sl 2 wyif.
Row 18: K 2 tog, k 1, pull right-most st on right-hand needle over nxt st for first BO. BO 4 more sts. Knit across (11 sts left).
Row 19: Sl 2 wyif, (p 1, k 1) 3 times, p 1, sl 2 wyif.

Row 20: K 2, ssk, k 3, k 2 tog, k 2.
Row 21: Sl 2 wyif, (p 1, k 1) 2 times, p 1, sl 2 wyif.
Row 22: K 2, ssk, k 1, k 2 tog, k 2.
Row 23: Sl 2 wyif, p 1, k 1, p 1, sl 2 wyif.
Row 24: K 2, s2sk, k 2. Wrap yarn twice around sts at base of needle. Turn.
Row 25: Sl 1 wyif, (m 1, p 1) 3 times, sl 1 wyif.
Tail: Work rows 26–39 on the first four sts, leaving rem sts on holder.
Row 26: K 2, m 1, k 2.
Row 27: Sl 2 wyif, m 1, p 1, m 1, sl 2 wyif.
Row 28: K 2, p 1, m 1, k 1, m 1, p 1, k 2.
Row 29: Sl 2 wyif, k 1, m 1, k 1, p 1, k 1, m 1, k 1, sl 2 wyif.
Row 30: K 2, (p 1, k 1) 3 times, p 1, k 2.
Row 31: Sl 2 wyif, (k 1, p 1) 3 times, k 1, sl 2 wyif.
Row 32: K 2, p 1, k 1, s2sk, k 1, p 1, k 2.
Row 33: Sl 2 wyif, k 1, p 3, k 1, sl 2 wyif.
Row 34: K 2, p 1, s2sk, p 1, k 2.
Row 35: Sl 2 wyif, k 1, p 1, k 1, sl 2 wyif.
Row 36: K 2, s2sk, k 2.
Row 37: Sl 2 wyif, p 1, sl 2 wyif.
Row 38: K 1, s2sk, k 1.
Row 39: P 3 tog. Fasten off.
Complete 2nd half of tail in same manner.

Shoulder seams: With right sides tog, having shoulder sts from back and front on separate needles, and with larger-size needle, k 2 tog the first st from each holder, * k tog the nxt st from each needle, BO; rep from * across until all sts are bound off. Rep for 2nd shoulder.
Button band: With right sides facing and with smaller needles, pick up and k 48 (50, 52, 56, 58) sts on edge to point where neck shaping begins, 38 (40, 42, 46, 48) sts to back of neck, work across 25 (25, 27, 27, 29) sts from back holder, 38 (40, 42, 46, 48) sts to point where neck shaping begins, 48 (50, 52, 56, 58) sts to lower edge—197 (205, 215, 231, 241) sts.
Row 1 (ws): P 1, * k 1, p 1; rep from *.
Row 2: K 1, * p 1, k 1; rep from *. Rep row 1 once more.

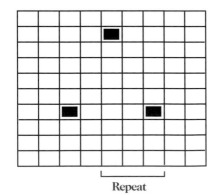

Repeat

CHART 1

Buttonhole row: K 1, p 1, k 1, * k 2 tog, yo, work in established rib for 6 (6, 6, 8, 8) sts; rep from * 4 times, k 2 tog, yo, work as established to end of row. Work rows 1 and 2 once more. BO in rib. Sew underarm sleeve seams and set in at armhole opening. Sew buttons opposite buttonholes.

Appliquéd and embroidered details: With kelly green and light green yarn, embroider seaweed on front and back of cardigan, using backstitching and long stitches and referring to photos on page **131** for placement. Glue ribbon to right-hand side of sweater, using photo as a guide for placement, catching in ¼" end of ribbon on wrong side of sweater just above ribbing, and folding ribbon under ⅛" at top edge. (**Note:** Plan to place one piece of ribbon over fish on right-hand side of sweater.) Repeat on left-hand side of sweater and on sweater back. Position fish on sweater front and back, referring to photos for placement, and sew in place, using Bright Pink yarn. Make French knot for eye on each fish, using Bright Pink yarn. Glue ribbon over fish on right-hand side of sweater.

Crazy-Quilt Vest

Materials:
Purchased vest pattern of your choice
Yardage required for vest pattern (**Note:** Choose cotton voile or other lightweight fabric for vest front.)
⅛–¼ yd. **each** of five different 44/45"-wide wool or wool-blend solids and prints
Thread to match fabrics
1¼ yds. Pellon® Wonder-Under® Transfer Web **or** Heat N Bond® fusible web
1 yd. **each** of four different ¼"–½"-wide trims of your choice
Three frog closures
Straight pins
Scissors
Iron
Sewing machine with zigzag stitch

Note: Materials listed will make one *Crazy-Quilt Vest.*

1. Cut vest-front pieces from cotton voile or lightweight cotton, using vest pattern. Set aside.
2. Fuse Wonder-Under® or Heat N Bond® to wrong side of wool or wool-blend fabrics, following manufacturer's instructions for fusing. Cut fabrics into assorted shapes to fit atop vest-front pieces, trimming away excess fabric as needed. Remove paper backing from fabric shapes and fuse shapes to right side of vest-front pieces.
3. Machine sew trims along raw edges of fabric shapes, using zigzag stitch.
4. Complete vest construction following instructions given with pattern. Sew frog closures to front of vest.

Holiday Ribbons Vest

Materials:
Black evenweave vest (**Note:** Designer used Hickory Hollow vest.)
1½ yds. ⅝"-wide dusty blue satin ribbon
1 yd. ⅝"-wide soft green satin ribbon
1 yd. ⅝"-wide burgundy satin ribbon
2 yds. ⅛"-wide soft green satin ribbon (cut into 1 yd. lengths)
1½ yds. ⅛"-wide pink double-face satin ribbon
1 skein **each** size 5 pearl cotton, colors: #605 pink, #104 variegated yellow
1 skein size 3 pearl cotton, color: #993 green
1 pkg. Mill Hill glass seed beads, color: #00128 yellow
1 pkg. Mill Hill small bugle beads, color: #72005 pink
Thread to match ribbons
Thread, color: black
Needles: hand-sewing with small eye, embroidery with large eye
Light-color dressmaker's carbon
Light-color marking pencil
Ruler **or** yardstick
Small piece of heavy cardboard (to slide into shoulders of vest while embroidering)
Seam sealant
Scissors
Iron
Straight pins (optional)
Thimble (optional)

1. Transfer pattern to vest, reversing for left-hand side and using dressmaker's carbon.
2. Sew each length of ⅛"-wide green ribbon to one side of vest atop vine pattern, using a running stitch and thread to match ribbon.
3. To make blue flowers, cut ten 5" lengths from blue ribbon. Fold each length of ribbon in half, placing right sides together and aligning ends. Sew ends together; then sew a running stitch along one long edge. Pull thread ends of running stitch to gather ribbon into a tight circle. Knot thread ends together; then sew across opening on back several times to secure. Sew one small yellow bead to center of flower.

Sew flowers to vest as indicated on pattern, using a small running stitch and thread to match ribbon.
4. To make burgundy flowers, cut four 6" lengths from burgundy ribbon. Fold each length of ribbon in half, placing right sides together and aligning ends. Sew ends together; then gather each piece in a zigzag pattern from one edge to the other. Pull thread ends to gather, flatten ribbon into a blossom, and then sew edges together at center. Knot securely. Sew three pink beads to flower center in a "Y" shape. Sew flowers to vest as indicated on pattern, using thread to match ribbon.
5. Cut remaining burgundy ribbon into six 2" lengths. Cut ends of each piece on the diagonal, cutting in opposite directions. Apply seam sealant to cut ends and let dry. Sew running stitch along one cut end, the short-side edge, and opposite cut end. (**Note:** Long-side edge will remain unsewn.) Gather thread tightly and knot ends to secure. Sew buds to vest.
6. To make large, pink daisies, mark a ⅜" circle for flower center and five ¾" lines radiating out from center for petals. Cut 1½ yd. length of pink ribbon in half. For each daisy, thread embroidery needle with pink ribbon and make lazy-daisy stitches on marked lines, taking care not to twist ribbon. Knot ribbon ends on back to secure. Thread needle with pearl cotton and make shorter lazy-daisy stitches between ribbon petals, taking one straight stitch to fill in center of each petal. Make French knots to fill in center of daisy, using yellow pearl cotton.
7. Cut four 3¼" lengths and six 2½" lengths from ⅝"-wide green ribbon. To make each pair of leaves, fold a piece of ribbon in half lengthwise, placing right sides of ribbon together. Sew across each short end, using a 3/16" seam allowance. Turn right-side out, forming a point on each end. Gather center of each leaf pair and sew to vest, placing large pairs of leaves on each side of daisies and small pairs of leaves as indicated on pattern.
8. Make three lazy-daisy stitches, using pink pearl cotton, to form each pink bud.
9. Make small lazy-daisy leaves along vine, using green pearl cotton. Work stems of pink buds in stem stitch, using green pearl cotton, and cover ends of pink buds with satin stitch worked with pink pearl cotton.
10. Sew two yellow beads at top of each pink bud, using black thread. Sew pink bugle beads randomly around flowers as indicated on pattern, using black thread.

HOLIDAY RIBBONS VEST PATTERN & STITCH ILLUSTRATIONS

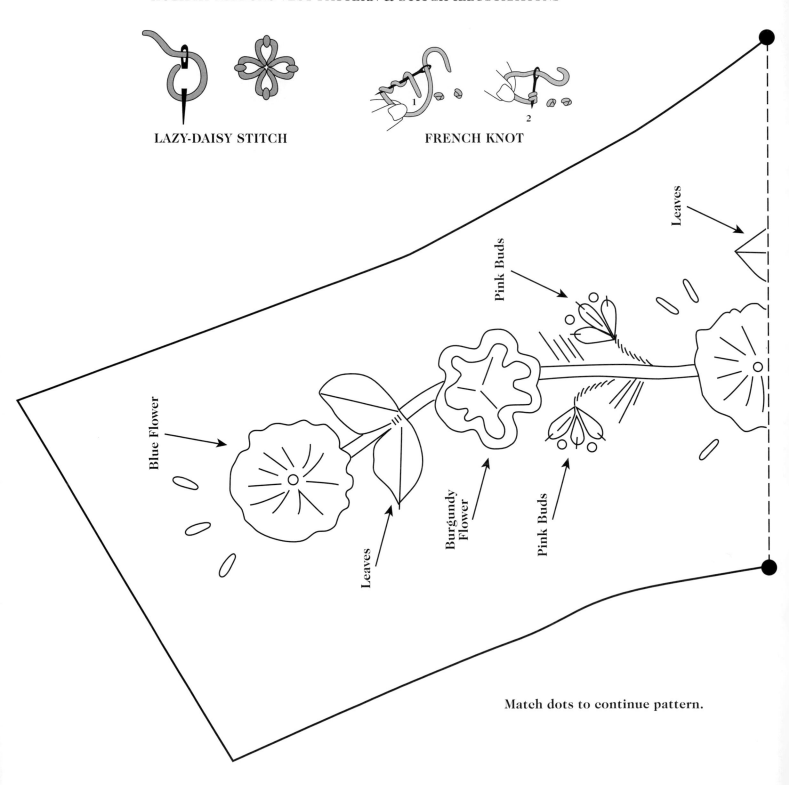

LAZY-DAISY STITCH

FRENCH KNOT

Leaves

Pink Buds

Blue Flower

Leaves

Burgundy Flower

Pink Buds

Match dots to continue pattern.

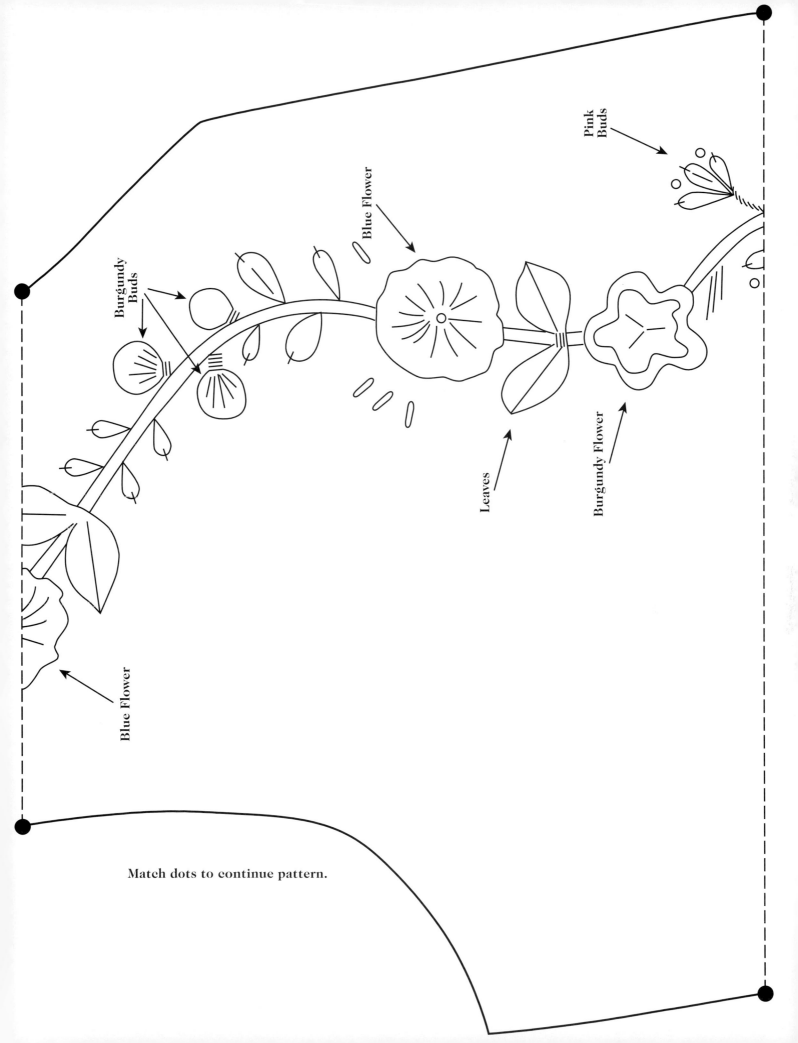

Pink
Buds

Blue Flower

Burgundy
Buds

Leaves

Burgundy Flower

Blue Flower

Match dots to continue pattern.

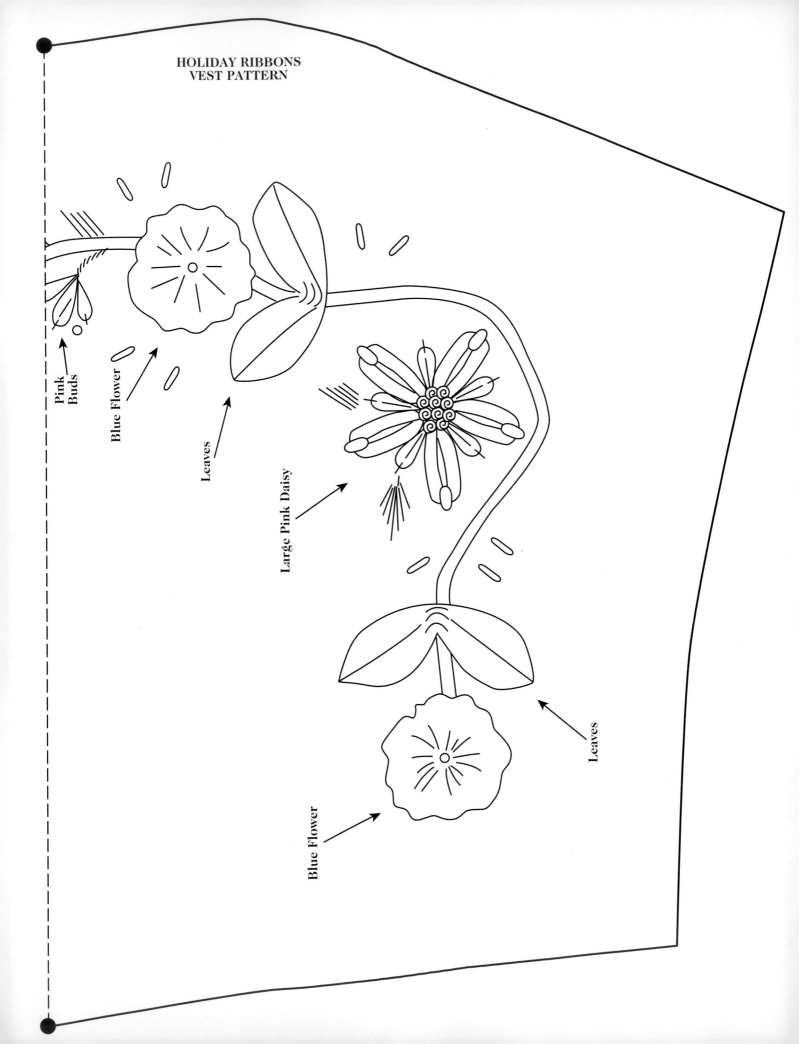

HOLIDAY RIBBONS
VEST PATTERN

Pink
Buds

Blue Flower

Leaves

Large Pink Daisy

Leaves

Blue Flower

Shopper's Guide

Cover
Fabric from Concord, courtesy of Calico Corners, Birmingham, Alabama.

Jewel-Tone Ornaments
Page 10—For catalog to order iron-on fabric silhouette squares, send $1 to Tree Toys, P.O. Box 492, Hinsdale, IL 60522-0492; for catalog to order transparent Gallery Glass™ paints, send $2 to Suncoast Discount Arts and Crafts, 9015 U.S. Highway 19 North, Penallas Park, FL 34666.

Foyer Tree
Page 18—Yarn Tree Designs needlework cards available from Keepsakes, 329 Main Street, Ames, IA 50010, 1-800-524-9694.

Candy-Stripe Place Mat Set
Page 43—*Original Christmas Tree* china by Cuthbertson; *Sheila* crystal by Waterford.

Black and White Table Toppers
Page 49—*Palazzo* china by Signature Housewares, Inc., courtesy of Rich's, Birmingham, Alabama.

Banister Trimmings
Page 67—Wire-edged ribbon available from W.F.R. Ribbon, Inc., 259 Center Street, Phillipsburg, NJ 08865-3397, 1-800-883-7700.

Doily Pillows
Page 110—Round Battenberg doilies from The Linen Lady, 885 57th St., Sacramento, CA 95819, (916) 457-6718.

House Buttons
Page 111—1½" ready-to-cover buttons from Hancock Fabrics, Birmingham, Alabama; red cardigan courtesy of Rich's, Birmingham, Alabama.

Ribbon and Bead Package Tags
Page 112—For a source for acrylic cabochons, contact The Beadery, P.O. Box 178, Hope Valley, RI 02832.

Papier Tole Snowman
Page 113—To order snowman silhouettes, No. 312, send $1.00 for catalog to Tree Toys, P.O. Box 492, Hinsdale, IL 60522-0492. For ordering information for Glass Kote and thinner, send SASE to Carolyn's Crafts, 4 Elk's Plaza Parkway, Box 142, Gatlinburg, TN 37738.

Holiday Ribbons Vest
Page 128—Black linen vest (#5003B—specify S, L, XL—$52.00 + $5.50 shipping & handling) available from Just CrossStitch®, 405 Riverhills Business Park, Birmingham, AL 35242, 1-800-768-5878.

Items not included in "Shopper's Guide" are either commonly available, antiques, or from private collections.

Basic Stitch Diagrams

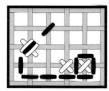

Backstitch (across two ¾ stitches and around full cross)

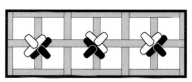

Two ¾ Stitches (in one square, using two different floss colors)

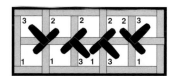

¾ Cross Stitches (over one in various positions)

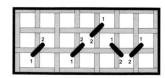

¼ Cross Stitch (over two threads)

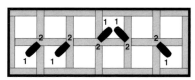

¼ Cross Stitch (over one thread)

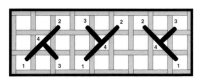

¾ Cross Stitch (over two threads)

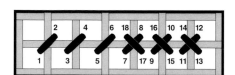

Full Cross Stitch (over one thread)

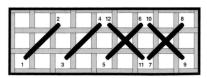

Full Cross Stitch (over two threads)

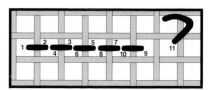

Basic Backstitch

French Knot

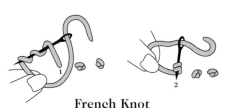

Backstitch (showing variations)

General Instructions for Cross Stitch

Basic Supplies: Even-weave fabric, tapestry needle(s), six-strand embroidery floss, embroidery scissors, embroidery hoop (optional).

Fabric Preparation: The instructions and yardage for finishing materials have been written and calculated for each of the projects shown stitched on the fabric listed in each color code. Alternate fabric choices have also been listed. If you wish to stitch a design on an alternate fabric, or alter its placement, you will need to recalculate the finished size of the project, as well as the yardage of finishing materials needed, and make the necessary dimension adjustments when finishing.

Determine size of fabric needed for a project by dividing number of horizontal stitches by thread count of fabric. For example, if a design 35 stitches wide is worked on 14-count fabric, it will cover 2½" (35 divided by 14 equals 2½). Repeat process for vertical count. Add three inches on all sides of design area to find dimensions for cutting fabric. Whipstitch edges to prevent fraying.

Floss Preparation: Cut floss into 14" to 18" lengths. Separate all six strands. Reunite number of strands needed and thread needle, leaving one floss end longer than the other.

Where to Start: Start wherever you like! Some designers suggest finding center of fabric and starting there. Others recommend beginning with a central motif, while still others work borders first. Many find fabric center, count up and back to the left, and start with the uppermost left stitch. Wherever you begin, be sure to leave allowance for all horizontal and vertical stitches so that a 3" fabric margin is left around completed design.

Should you choose to begin at the center point, find it by folding fabric from top to bottom and then from left to right. Use a straight pin to mark upper-left corner at junction of folds, and then unfold fabric. Pin will be in center of fabric.

After deciding where to begin on fabric, find same point on graph. Each square on graph represents one stitch. Those squares containing a symbol (i.e., X,T,O) indicate that a stitch should be made in that space over those threads. Different symbols represent different colors of floss for stitches. (See color code of chart.) They may also indicate partial or decorative stitches. Familiarize yourself with color code before you begin stitching. Even-weave fabric may be stretched over an embroidery hoop to facilitate stitching.

Stitching the Design: Using the diagrams on page 141, stitch design, completing all full and partial cross stitches first. Cross all full cross stitches in same direction to achieve a smooth surface appearance. Work backstitches second, and any decorative stitches last.

Helpful Hints for Stitching: Do not knot floss. Instead, catch end on back of work with first few stitches. As you stitch, pull floss through fabric "holes" with one stroke, not several short ones. The moment you feel resistance from floss, cease pulling. Consistent tension on floss results in a smoother look for stitches. Drop your needle frequently to allow floss to untwist. It twists naturally as you stitch and, as it gets shorter, must be allowed to untwist more often. To begin a new color on project, prepare floss and secure new strands as noted. To end stitching, run floss under several completed stitches and clip remaining strands close to surface.

Many times it is necessary to skip a few spaces (threads) on the fabric in order to continue a row of stitches in the same color. If you must skip an area covering more than ¼", end stitching as described and begin again at next point. This procedure prevents uneven tension on the embroidery surface and snagging on the back. It also keeps colors from showing through unstitched areas. Do not carry thread over an area that will remain unstitched.

When You Are Finished: For designs using cotton or linen floss on cotton or linen even-weave fabric, hand wash piece with mild detergent in warm water. Rinse thoroughly with cold water. Roll in terry towel and squeeze gently to remove excess moisture. Do not wring. Unroll towel and allow piece to dry until barely damp. Iron on padded surface with design face down, using medium setting for heat. A press cloth will help prevent shine on dark fabrics. **Note:** Acrylics, acrylic blends, wools, or silks must be treated differently when cleaning. Check manufacturer's guidelines for special cleaning instructions.

Helpful Hints for Crafting

The instructions and yardage for finishing materials have been written and calculated for each of the projects shown and crafted from the materials listed. If you wish to craft a design using materials of different dimensions than those listed or to stitch a design on an alternate fabric or to alter its placement, you will need to recalculate the finished size of the project, as well as the yardage of finishing materials needed, and make the necessary dimension adjustments when purchasing supplies and making the projects.

Crafters and Designers

Index

Numbers in **bold** type indicate color photo pages. All other numbers refer to pages for charts, color codes, patterns, and instructions.